Ayelet Segal

Telos

From Theory to Practice
A Voyage on the Way to Ascension

Guided by Adama -Telos High Priest
and Other Entities of Light

Ayelet Segal

Telos
From Theory to Practice
A Voyage on the Way to Ascension
Guided by Adama – Telos High Priest
and Other Entities of Light

Translation: Susan Rosenfeld
Editing: MT Shasta Light Publishing
Photographer: Victoria Lee
Design : Leanne Zinkand Silverlining Designs
Cover Design: Michael Teva

Copyright © 2014 by Ayelet Segal

ISBN: 978-1540630230

All rights reserved. No part of this book may be translated, reproduced, stored in a retrieval system or transmitted, in any form or by any means, electronic, photocopying, recording or otherwise, without prior permission in writing from the author

*To my parents, Pearl and Judah Diamant,
who gave me their love and the breath of life.
Saar, my beloved husband, his patience gave me the
freedom to journey.
And to dear Victoria, my mentor who accompanied me
on my journey's way to Telos.*

Dedication

I dedicate this book to all the souls awakening at this time to the new age.

To all whose hearts vibrate with the frequency of love, to all who are on the journey to the light, the journey of life—the eternal life of the soul.

I dedicate this book to all the inhabitants of the Middle East who yearn for a serene and harmonious life, who yearn for a life of action, creation, and love.

I dedicate this book to the High Priest, Adama, who has accompanied me on the most exciting journey of my life; to the beloved children of Telos; to the exalted masters; to my friend Duniyao and to all the people of the marvelous light city.

Thanks

Thanks to the Creator of the World, who opened before me the gates of heaven.

Thanks to the High Priest Adama, who accompanies me throughout my journey of ascendance.

Thanks to the masters for their supreme wisdom.

Thanks to the children of Telos and all the marvelous beings from the light city Telos.

Deep thanks to my companions on the journey in all dimensions, for enveloping me in love and supporting me.

I thank the members of the Telos-Israel community for their giving and for the shared creation for the sake of the planet and for the sake of creating unity, harmony, and love for humankind.

Thanks to members of Telos throughout the world who have supported the publishing of the book and encouraged me in the process, and who support me as Lemurian brothers on the shared journey.

Thanks to Miri Arad for her professional editing and for the energetic connection between us.

Thanks to Simona and Michael of Galim Publishing for their support, their patience, and their belief in the importance of the knowledge and its dissemination.

Table of Contents

Preface: My personal story: 2010 11
Greeting from Adama 19

Part I
The Enlightenment of the Middle East 25

The Story of the Middle East 26
The Role of the Jews in the Middle East 34
The Importance of Light Work and its Dissemination
in the Middle East 39
Message from Master Sananda 44
Message from Saint Germain 46
The Gulf of Eilat—Meditation
I take a deep breath and enter a meditative state. 48

Part II
Between Dimensions 51

New Times 52
Passage between the Dimensions 55
Energetic Gateways 58
The Gateway of November 11, 2011 60
"Big Brother" 64
Survey of Reality 67
Japan 72

Part III
Telos 77

A Visit to the Light City Telos 78
The Buildings in Telos 80

The Upper Light Cities	85
A Journey of Healing to the Light City Luxor	88
The Process of Emerging from the Mountain	93
Friends from Another Star	95
Extraterrestrial Beings	99
Meeting with the Pleiadians	103
Conversation with the commander of the Pleiadian spaceship	105
The Sixth Level	108
Meditation: a Visit to the Sixth Level	110
The Golden Flame	113
The Flame of Harmony	119
The New Children	127
Message from Matirion, a Mature Child from Telos	131
Transmitting Information: the Children of Light	133
Education	135
A Trip Around Telos: Meeting the Children	140
The Role of Women	146
Message from Lady Nada	150
Meditation: Temple of the Priestesses	152
The Energy of Sex	155
The Energetic Connection–the Explosion of Love	161
Balancing Sex Energy: Lesson 1	164
The Temple of Sexual Energy	168
Meditation for the Temple of Union	177
The Temple of Union Meditation: the Last Step	180
The Crystal City	188

Part IV

The Journey of Ascension 195
The Game of Enlightenment: the Stage of Ascension 196
The Acceleration of Time 202
Planetary Changes 204
Message from the Light Entity Gabrielo about Planetary Changes 207
Change in the Frequency of Mother Earth 209
Temple of the Dolphins 212
Meditation with the Dolphins 214
From Theory to Practice 217
The Changes in Our Bodies 222
Joining the Light Bodies 225
Meditation: Connecting the Bodies 228
The Stages in the Journey of Awakening 230
Activating DNA 235
Rules of the Light Disseminator 238
The Human Genome 242
Strengthening of the Way 245
Who is the Master? 247
Leadership 252
Giving 254
The Awakening of the Golden Age 257
2014–a year of spiritual maturity. 258
Reaching Our Personal Purpose in the Golden age 260
11 Steps for Finding the Purpose 264

Part V
The Code for Peace 267
The First Code: The Kingdom Chakra 270

The Second Code: The Crown Chakra 273
The Third Code: The Third Eye Chakra 275
The Fourth Code: the Throat Chakra 277
The Fifth Code: the Heart Chakra 279
The Sixth Code: the Chakra of the Solar Plexus 281
The Seventh Code: the Sacral Chakra 282
The Eighth Code: the Sex Chakra 285
The Ninth Code: the Silver Chakra 287
The Tenth Code: the Gold Chakra 289
Peace 290
The Turquoise Flame: the Peace Flame 293
Inner Peace: A Message from Aurelia Louise Jones 299
Glossary 303

Books published by Ayelet Segal 312

About Ayelet Segal 314

Preface

My personal story: 2010

Mt. Shasta changed my life. I knew this a year earlier when I closed the book, *Telos, Volume 2, Messages for the Enlightenment of a Humanity in Transformation,* by Aurelia Louise Jones, author of the Telos Book Series telling the story of the City of Light, Telos.

Two months before my thirty-fifth birthday, I received a gift from my older brother: a ticket to fly to the U.S. for the wedding of friends. It was clear to me that the wedding was a cover for the true purpose of the trip—a visit to Mt. Shasta. Deep in my heart, I knew I was about to have the experience of my life on the mountain.

The day before my birthday, I arrived in the town of Mount Shasta in northern California, where I was received by four angels in human form. The angels were representatives of Telos-USA who had come to meet me, a representative of Telos-Israel, an organization still taking shape at that time. The angels knew how to make me feel comfortable and create a sense of calm and great love.

After indulging ourselves at a charming restaurant, we held our first meditation in one of their homes.

This meditation was visited by the spirit of Master St. Germain. In the course of the meditation, all who were present entered the mountain crater by means of an etheric chariot. We followed a guide who led us to a pool of water in an enchanting natural stream. Entering a crystal cave, we continued behind the guide as he led us to a lift, which took us into the depths of the earth.

Six chairs awaited us there. In the sixth chair sat St. Germain, and it was he who gave us a message. His message was that we must continue the wonderful work we were doing for humanity, for nature, and for Planet Earth. We were told that the people of the city of Telos were working toward the enlightenment of the world and raising the level of consciousness, that we must continue the light work in which we were engaged. It was a warm and cordial message. I remember how, during the channeling, Aurelia's cat, Angelo, came to us and began conversing with the Master.

On Monday morning, my thirty-fifth birthday, we met again in order to conduct an ascension ceremony of spiritual expression of intentions. The ceremony was very powerful, and moved me to tears. In the room stood a chair draped in golden cloth; on the table were pictures of the High Priest Adama, of Master St. Germain, of Master Serapis Bey, and also of Aurelia. The ceremony opened with a prayer and the masters were invited in, and all present took turns sitting on the chair and expressing their intentions. As I sat on the chair, I felt my body becoming warmer and my heart expanding. I expressed my intention to work for humanity, to illuminate the awakening of humanity, and to give of my life to this goal. I expressed my intentions in Hebrew, and in closing even said a certain prayer–although I don't know how and from where I knew it, since my upbringing was strictly secular.

I left the ceremony greatly moved, still unable to assimilate all the expansion that had taken place in such a short time. I recall that the friends from Telos-USA urged me to make haste and reach the mountain, because I must undergo something important there. I felt they knew something I didn't...

They took me to a store for camping gear, where I bought equipment to hike on the snow-covered mountain. We then set off for the mountain. My excitement was growing, and although I didn't know what lay in store for me, I was sure this was going to be the most wonderful birthday I had ever had.

We drove higher and higher up the mountain, with some two and a half meters of snow lining parts of the road. The friends who were with me said it had been snowing incessantly until the day before, and I felt that the snow had actually stopped falling in my honor. The sun was out, smiling down from a clear, cloudless sky. I took leave of my friends and climbed the mountain. With special walking shoes and support poles, I ascended higher and higher, singing to myself. I reached a flat platform and wondered where I should go from there.

I noticed a further ascent to a higher area, and in my climbing boots and snow shoes, I headed in that direction, singing a cheerful song I made up on this wonderful day.

The sun shone. I climbed and climbed, and when I arrived, I sat down overlooking the crater of the mountain, opposite an enormous pine tree. My heart rate accelerated from the strenuous climb, then returned to normal and my body grew calm. The connection was immediate; the vibrations in my body rose rapidly.

Then a dragon named Orelio arrived and took me on his wings. At first, I was fearful, but very soon felt the freedom of rapid flight. We flew up above the trees and above the mountain, circled the mountain a few times, then entered it and came out of it several times. An enormous smile spread over my face. Orelio took me into the mountain and brought me to a room sparkling with crystals. There we parted, but not before he had sent a pink ray of love to my heart. I felt free, calm, and happy.

My heart chakra opened completely, and tears flowed from my eyes. The love of the fifth dimension began to penetrate my heart. Then Adama appeared in all his glory. He stood before me with twinkling eyes and said, "We are happy with the wonderful work you have done in such a short time." He told me to sit on a sparkling chair made of crystal, and I entered a trance until my breathing almost stopped. Only a fine thread held me; immense energy entered me through my crown chakra, and my entire body trembled. I felt an orgasm throughout my body; all the cells in my body opened. The energy continued flowing for several moments. I have no words to describe the intensity of that feeling.

"You will bring this energy to the world at large: to children, to women, to nature, to humanity. This is your role;

you have been born anew. Your life has changed; this is your choice," he said. I received a message to continue my work in education in order to help the crystal children and the indigo children, while at the same time building the center.

When the energy stopped flowing, a bright white light flashed. I felt love and serenity. I began to cry with a sense of liberation. I felt tremendous thankfulness to Adama, to Orelio, and to God, as well as a commitment to spread the light during my physical life on earth.

The first thing I did upon opening my eyes was to write down my experience, and I am most grateful to Victoria for urging me to take along pen and paper, and to write. Since that day, I have felt in my bones the desire to spread the vibrations of love and light that I experienced on the mountain, and to continue working in complete cooperation with Adama and with the masters who, step by step, are leading the expansion of Telos-Israel.

Upon my return to Israel, I began to fulfill the mission I had undertaken when I was on the mountain. My arrival landed me back in the reality of the third dimension—work, family, and friends. The landing was not easy, and I continued to float in the enjoyment of the energies of Shasta.

I must note that from the very beginning, all the predictions I received have materialized—and here is a wonderful example: while on the mountain, I was told that I would give birth to a daughter (I had three sons at the time). Indeed, I very soon became pregnant for the fourth time, and, as I was told on the mountain, was granted a daughter—proof of the existence and realization of the words of the High Priest Adama.

The journey to Telos takes place on a path of absolute faith, a path on which the connection to the sacred heart is essential, a path on which one deals with challenging lessons. Today I am aware how far those lessons have taken me on my personal spiritual journey, as well as on my journey as part of Telos-Israel.

One day during that period, I felt the urge to go to the sea. I wrote at the time in my notebook:

"I sit facing the sea, which calms me and detaches me from the confusion between reality and imagination, between the third dimension, which is the material dimension, and the fifth dimension that is in my imagination."

My life did indeed change. My soul opened to the secrets of the universe, to the new age, to inner awakening. There are no words to describe the scale of the sublime experience I have undergone, which flows within me and makes me feel endless longing for home, for the place where everything began long before I bravely chose to enter the cycles of free choice.

Lemuria—enchanted continent, paradise of truth, of joy, and of so much love. At present there are only hints, sparks of light trying to enter blocked human memory—blocked by choice. The difficulty of continuing to play the game is enormous, and fleeing to the imagination does not always help; yet the magic exists and so does the reason, so the "great performer" carries on playing out the scenes of life.

I see in this a mission. How does a light worker illuminate the unawakened? With a great deal of determination and charisma—but ultimately the choice is theirs to make, through their own free will.

There on the mountain, when everything was open, serene, peaceful, and loving, it was clear to me again, for a split second, why I had returned. I was taken on a journey to Telos, a journey in time where I met my Lemurian family and connected to my existence in the City of Light, Telos. That in itself, was a powerful experience. A strong ray of light illuminated me, and I met the noble, strong figure of Adama. Adama presented himself as my father, a beautiful and accepting figure. I am surrounded by love from them all, and know they are at my side, helping, supporting, and communicating.

Today I choose again to live my life as Ayelet, mother to my children and partner to my husband, in the paradise in which I live. I choose to bestow unconditional love on humanity and to contribute to raising human consciousness.

Thank you, dear ones. Thank you, Ayelet.

Greeting from Adama

Good evening and welcome. This is Adama, High Priest of Telos, welcoming you.

We are happy to convey to you at this time the energy that will open your hearts and connect you with the ancient knowledge that is within you. This knowledge will guide you, human beings, on the spiritual path in the third dimension in which you exist. The game goes on, time is progressing, and we are with you at this time, through the cooperation of the sons of light that exist in the higher dimensions with the sons of light in the dense third dimension, who are open to receiving the divine light.

The dimension in which you live is still dense and full of hardship; these hardships sometimes cause you to lose connection with the supreme creator and return to working in an automatic way, without opening the heart. You are accustomed to functioning through the brain, but the brain cannot connect you to the higher dimensions because these dimensions must be accessed through the heart; it must be done without ego, without judgment, without competitiveness and without the personal agenda so characteristic of human beings. Connection with the higher dimensions must be from that sacred place: the connection with the creator of the world who is both your father and your mother, who created and is still creating all the creatures that exist in the present universe and in parallel universes.

My dear ones, we in the city of light, Telos, are happy to see the people of ancient Lemuria awakening to the memories and to the light, the light in which we lived in harmony in a bygone age, before the sinking of the continent. This is the light that exists in the families of your soul–those who still live in Lemuria, on the planet of Lemuria, full of light and created out of a feeling of love and harmony. These Lemurians live lives whose purpose is to plant the seeds of love from which all the races of humanity were created. My dear ones, today the light illuminates almost ninety percent of the planet. We are not satisfied with this, however, and continue to work so that this universe and all parallel universes will be in the light.

Know that at this time, many are arriving from stars that exist in distant universes in order to observe the awakening of humanity and the changes the planet is undergoing. Many different peoples and races are interested in the change and feel that the desire to live in harmony, love, and peace is at its greatest and most powerful intensity in the history of humanity. This experience will be realized as the sons of light continue to awaken; thus, the joy is great in Telos and in many other cities of light on the planet.

Have you visited the cities of light found beneath the pyramids of Egypt recently? Have you visited the light cities beneath the monasteries of Tibet or those in South America? In all of them, there are light entities engaged in enlightening the earth and in creating balance among all living above ground; the tempo of their work is accelerating as time accelerates even more; the planet is revolving faster than in the past (soon your scientists will have questions about the earth's rotation on its axis and it's revolution around the sun) and the seasons of the year are changing. The familiar is disappearing and the new that is being created every day is taking its place.

We in Telos are working in places that are important energetic portals with light groups from all over the planet, including sons and daughters of Lemuria and sons and daughters of Telos. We invite you to visit our temples and their many levels of healing. Come with your children, and see for yourselves that through a link between your children and the children of Telos, knowledge of the light will arise in your children. Some light entities incarnated on earth at this time find themselves caught on the astral plane and come to us for treatment and day-to-day instruction in the ways of light. We invite you to meet with the masters and learn how to reform your organizations in their struggle for light, justice, and equality.

This is a time of change among the sons of light, in which the new will push aside the old. Your communities will be broken down and built anew, and the new energy will enter the dark places and enlighten them. All societies, which are today damaged, will undergo transformation to become supporting and loving communities in which the strong support the weak, the happy embrace those who are sad, and the optimistic encourage those who are pessimistic.

This period will bring great innovation to Planet Earth. Over the years, we have developed an underground network of life based on light and love and energies whose source is the supreme creator. Today we are connected to all the cities of earth that exist underground and now is the time for their unveiling. The network of these cities was established with the support of angels and light entities from many levels. Indeed, fairly quickly, many entities on Planet Earth have awakened, and awakened both those in the cluster with whom they incarnated into this life, as well as those in their circles of influence. It is important to reach as many entities as possible; we invite you and will help you to "synchronize" with these light entities to expand and radiate the light together.

The purpose of this book is to speak of the enlightenment in the Middle East, and to make clear the importance of those light entities who have made the unique journey to connect with the Lemurian energy of love that exists throughout the world.

I, Adama, who represent the light people in Telos, see this mission as supremely important in order to raise the vibration of Planet Earth. A great leap forward will happen when the inhabitants of the area understand that there is only one way that works, and that is the way of the heart.

Part I

The Enlightenment of the Middle East

The souls in the region yearn for peace between the two peoples, the Ishmaelite [1] and the Jewish—and peace will indeed come.

---

[1] According to the Book of Genesis, Ishmaelites are the descendants of Ishmael, the elder son of Abraham

The Story of the Middle East

This is Adama, the High Priest of Telos, welcoming you.

The Middle East is one of the first regions to have been created on Planet Earth, and it is one of its energetic portals. The area had abundant rivers, streams, trees, and wildlife. Great knowledge was stored in the depths of the earth and in the mountains, among them the reddish mountains of Edom and Sinai, the first range to have been formed in the region. There were crystals deep in the earth that vibrated and influenced the entire landscape. However, the human beings in the region were not connected to the vibration of the light or the crystals, and eventually, over the years, the crystals were extinguished.

The story of the Middle East begins in the most ancient of times. Prehistoric man settled in the area, followed by primitive tribes that had not undergone evolutionary development and were completely cut off from the divine source.

When it was decided to settle light entities on earth, the only planet of choice, light entities arrived from many different planets and universes in order to awaken the planet, to integrate into the primitive tribes and to realize the vision of the Garden of Eden. The intention was to establish a society-colony of the planet Hodiya, and from it to learn about the possibility of free choice and about faith in the power of the creator. Among the light entities that arrived in the region were the Lemurians, followed by Abraham and Judah.

The first people of Hodiya to arrive began to put down roots. A small society of people from the planet lived in the area of the Dead Sea, beneath which there is a particularly powerful crystal that helped them in the early days to keep their small community alive.

At the same time, additional entities reached the planet from other stars. Some of them settled in the area known today as Saudi Arabia, where they maintained a great civilization. Another group of entities settled in what is known today as Iran, to study the planet and engage in personal learning, with the intention of returning this knowledge to their home star.

Unlike these groups, the people of Hodiya came to Planet Earth to settle permanently. These light entities wanted to spread the light into the region and practice their beliefs through study and the connection with God. Light entities at the time were powerful because they possessed divine knowledge; their purpose was not to use their power to rule, however, but to bestow love and to build a new society for coming generations—a society that would exist on the only planet of choice, so that each soul could follow its personal path and develop in accordance with the divine will designed for it.

Evolutionary development continued, meanwhile, and the tribespeople began to encounter the light entities. The tribespeople saw light entities as having special powers; they followed them blindly and worshipped them. Thus, the belief in deities began to develop.

The sons of light, not wanting to be worshipped, tried to teach the tribespeople to believe in the god within themselves. The tribespeople were not connected to this inner place, however, because prehistoric people were not yet highly evolved enough to hold this awareness.

As I have mentioned, Abraham too, arrived on the planet. Abraham was a great master; the purpose of his coming was to inculcate and intensify the light in human society. He came with perfect faith and a deep sense that his mission was to reawaken the light entities, who, in mingling and integrating with the tribespeople, had undergone a gradual decrease in their level of consciousness.

After Abraham, came additional messengers who disseminated and preserved the light. There were also periods in which much of humanity "closed their eyes" and fell to the third dimension of consciousness. During those periods, life in the third dimension was not easy; without technology, without progress, and without the spirit of God in their hearts, human beings began to perform acts that contradicted the vibrations of love, without compassion or giving. The vibrational level declined, even though masters arrived from time to time to restore them.

One of these masters was Jesus. His purpose was to endow humanity anew with the high vibration of compassion and love; however, he was unable to accomplish this mission and was obliged to ascend into a light body. Throughout history, the Jewish people have taken part in spreading the light. The Jews kindled the flame of God through their laws and their spiritual customs. As long as the temple existed, they continued their light work, which had a beneficial effect on the souls who were choosing to incarnate on earth.

Over time, most of the tribes became integrated into the colonies of the Sons of light and humanity was rebuilt. Souls continued to arrive on the planet for the purpose of self-learning in free choice. Some were able to maintain a more open consciousness, to connect with their "higher selves" and to realize their true capabilities. Among such souls were Mozart, Newton, Einstein, Buddha, Gandhi, and many others whose unique qualities are recorded in history.

The Middle East region has known much suffering; aggressive wars for control and power have created negative energies that have spread throughout the world. On the one hand, the Middle East, particularly Eretz Yisrael[2], has been a spiritual center of attraction. The three monotheistic religions were created here. and it is rich in crystals that once vibrated with great intensity. Eretz Yisrael, on the other hand, has been a key region in the link between east and west, and many rulers have wanted to dominate it in order to control the world. Despite the darkness in which the area has existed for many generations, it is important

---

2 The Land of Israel

to realize that its geographical location and its being one of the energetic portals on Planet Earth, make emergence from the darkness a possibility.

Indeed, with the awakening today of many light entities in the area, a fundamental change is coming about. The awakening process of the crystals has already begun. Mother Earth is already preparing herself to absorb the new energy in the area. For some time now, energies and light rays of various intensities and purposes have been entering the region with the intention of awakening its inhabitants. But remember, dear human beings, that the final result depends on you—only through you can Mother Earth carefully and efficiently absorb these powerful energies. It is you who know how to absorb these strong energies and channel the knowledge to the right people—to those who will guide people to live lives of harmony, love, and the desire to return to the ideal that once existed on earth.

As you see, wars, conquest, suffering, control, enslavement and death are all are part of the human story. We, the forces of light, light entities who have realized the full potential of the star, seek to restore to it the vibrations of the era of harmony. Today, with you, we have the opportunity to accomplish this.

After the sinking of Lemuria, some of the priests, masters and other light entities decided to flee to Mt. Shasta, located in a region relatively close to the Mother continent. We were familiar with the area of the mountain, and thousands of years before the sinking, we had prepared it to take us all in with our children and family members.

When we arrived at the mountain, we could move between the fifth and the third dimensions without difficulty. The mountain was devoid of humans; it was all wilderness and beauty. When we arrived, we began to impart the legacy of the continent to our children. We taught them its history and carried on with our lives as if we were still in Lemuria.

The light bodies in which we chose to live underwent changes. Within the mountain, we began to build cities, villages, and places of purification, such as temples, alongside the natural sources of purification. Lakes and places abounding in crystals were the source of vitality within the mountain; without the crystals, it would have been impossible to maintain the cities of light.

We also organized a community system that supported and assisted the day-to-day functioning of the community, a system based on giving, harmony, love, trust, and the ability to work as a team. In this way, we managed to run the city of light, and here our children were born. Some of them decided to remain in the mountain, some went to work in the service of the deity in other galaxies, and others left the mountain and are assimilated among you.

This is what brave Aurelia Louise Jones did when she decided to give of herself for the good of humanity. For that, we are grateful to her and thank her.

We learned how to maintain contact with other light cities located across the globe, in places such as Egypt, South America, the area of Tibet, and the Middle East. Know that there still exist among you many Lemurian beings on the surface of the earth; they are fulfilling their mission by leading the process of raising humanity's vibration.

Over the years, we have witnessed volcanic eruptions, migration of tribes, and geological changes, as well as the arrival of the white man. For tens of thousands of years, we helped our Native brothers to safeguard the mountain. To this day, we are grateful to these brave tribes who protected us and who fought to keep the area pure and free from occupation.

We later encountered the people who had arrived from the European continent with blocked hearts. It was not easy to see them in the condition they were in, severed from their divine abilities, and ruled by the material greed that exists in the third dimension.

The "game"[3] on the planet of choice goes on, and is gaining momentum, and more light entities are joining it. This is the only planet on which the soul chooses for itself the events it will undergo; it chooses what to learn and what to develop, without help from the creator, without seeing the truth, but rather by groping in the dark.

An interesting detective game, isn't it? Would you like to take part in it? Of course you would—that is why you are still here, after living through many incarnations. The planet is growing in human population; mankind is developing and gaining insights. Beginning with the onset of the age of technology in the 19th century, the pace of technological development began to accelerate, and from primitive tribes you became an "enlightened civilization," as you call humanity. Yet conquest, wars, killing, and destruction continue to be part of the world of the human race.

---

3 "the game"– the Choosing of the Soul to reach planet Earth and to participate in the "game" free choice

In the late 1980's, a decision was made to continue enlightening and moving humanity forward toward change. The change did indeed begin, and is still ongoing. Humanity has been chosen to continue to maintain itself on the only planet of choice—but only if it successfully passes into the fifth dimension. Mother Earth has suffered a great deal in the third dimension and this period is ending; hence, we are taking an active part in raising the vibration of human beings and reconnecting them to the Lemurian heart, to the frequency of love and the ability to live in joy, love, and generosity.

The Role of the Jews in the Middle East

I am glad for this moment of unique cooperation in which we and the light entities who work with us, transmit relevant information to the many people joining the light in this special time. Light at present constitutes cosmic energy of great importance. Through it, we and the light entities can illuminate the planet, and eventually the entire universe.

These are messianic times, in which all light entities, both those in light bodies and those in human bodies, are choosing to reconnect to the higher self and to their primal bond with the Creator. In the third dimension, each divine spark has its own particular outer characteristic, and you human beings are now aware of the possibility of reconnecting to the Creator and to the forces of light that have been encoded in your etheric and physical bodies for ages.

As we have explained in previous books about Telos, those in light bodies first descended to earth in order to play a game. In this game, they established light colonies, and each colony chose to follow a path of developing consciousness.

The time during which they placed the crystal seeds in the depths of Mother Earth was the beginning era; they arrived in large and powerful light bodies, and generally lived between the fifth dimension and the third dimensions; but, of course, were able to rise beyond the fifth dimension with ease. At a certain time, light entities arriving from different stars and galaxies sought to take over the planet in order to exploit its store of knowledge. Thus began the wars for domination, which continued until the Creator put an end to them.

As a result, it was decided that, although the game on the only planet of choice would continue, every light entity who wanted to participate, would descend to the planet in complete forgetfulness, without consciousness. Thus, each light entity would experience the lessons of its soul, and every soul would make its own way toward spiritual growth. There were those souls who fell into the abyss and no longer wanted to be reborn on the planet, while many others continued to arrive from distant galaxies to take part in the game.

It came about that some regions on Planet Earth began to develop, while other areas remained in darkness. We must point out once again, that ever since the first colonies began to form, the region of the Middle East was a point of light and a gateway for many light entities. Throughout the different eras, many masters came to the area, and eventually the monotheistic religions developed here in sacred Jerusalem.

From the first settlement on earth by sons of light from the planet Hodiya, an especially large crystal was planted beneath the place from which the three religions grew, in order to enlighten and to transform negative energies into positive ones. The Temple was built above the crystal, with the Holy Ark at its center, so that a link was created between the energetic connections in the holy place below and the creators of the world above.

Over time, after the Second Temple was destroyed and the work of the clergy, the priests and the Levites, began to disintegrate, the crystal became inactive. Today, we are reactivating it with the help of many light groups who are working to bring vibrations of love, balance, and harmony to the region.

Many crystals were planted in different regions on earth, most beneath energetic portals that constitute entryways to the planet. In these areas, light colonies have been formed. Most of the crystals that were buried, have not been revealed to human beings, and will remain hidden in the future. Today, the recharging of all the crystals throughout the world is beginning, so it is very important for light workers on the planet to create a flow of energy from within their hearts that will maintain the effect of the crystals' operation on the earth's surface.

The Jewish people play a most important part in the game of light on the only planet of choice. When they arrived on the planet, the Jews established a colony in the Middle East, centered in the Jerusalem hills and in Jerusalem itself. They built a city of light, long before King David made Jerusalem the center of his kingdom. Their city of light in Jerusalem existed in the fifth dimension, and in their first game, Jewish light entities passed from dimension to dimension. Later, when the decision was made to reduce the conscious level of human beings, most Jewish souls who chose to be incarnated descended into the third dimension. The Jews have always received guidance from many sources of light—kings of light, angels, prophets, messengers and masters of the white brotherhood—who have also enlightened the region as a whole.

Despite many attempts to destroy the Jews, the Jewish religion has survived and the Jewish people exist to this day. This is by virtue of divine will, by virtue of the strong belief in their hearts, and by virtue of their having safeguarded the principles and values of their religion. Jews have a unique genetic code inherent in their DNA. This code characterizes the Jewish race, and a soul who chooses to be born as a Jew, must possess integrity and perseverance. Most souls who chose to incarnate as Jews succeed in this; however, there are also those who do not adhere to these rules and sin against the higher soul. These souls cannot be reincarnated as Jews.

The Jewish people, living today in their own state, continue to embody the light energy in the world. There will always be attempts to destroy them, but they receive protection so they can continue with their enlightenment and the enlightenment of the region.

I call upon the Jewish people to persist in their integrity, in giving, in sharing, in tolerance, in love, in compassion and in truthfulness. The spiritual collective of the Jewish people chose the lesson of the Holocaust in order to rid themselves of negative karma and to make a great leap in enlightening human existence and bringing about the ascension of the entire planet. In this choice, there was immense sacrifice and a great collective lesson.

The home stars of the Jews and the Lemurians are connected at the level of will and persistence in the global mission; they arrived on the planet in order to enlighten it and create a new home in the game of free choice. Indeed, they have planted on Mother Earth many seeds of light that guide humanity on the path of a harmonious and light-filled life; many light entities from both stars have joined together to create an enduring connection, thus opening up possibilities for passage between the two wonderful light groups. In fact, many of you who feel the Lemurian vibrations were previously Jews, and vice versa.

The Importance of Light Work and its Dissemination in the Middle East

At this time, dear ones, knowledge is available in light from many different directions. Channeling reaches you from the places we choose intentionally in order to make you understand that knowledge is accessible to all. We want each and every one of you light entities to become stronger, to open your hearts, and to carry out the mission of light from the cleanest, purest place within. In these times, there is no room for ego, control, or competitiveness; we are all one, and the mission before us is to raise the vibration on the surface of the planet.

As I have mentioned, the Middle East is of great importance in intensifying the process. Many beings in the region are filled with hatred, and one of the tasks of the masters and the light entities is to bring about a rapid transformation that will open the hearts of dormant light beings—Jews, Muslims, and Christians—who live here as neighbors.

Very soon, as the entities of darkness who have used force to gain control leave the "game of free choice" on earth, new leaders will arise from among the people and from within the light to bring about change. In order for the light energy to increase in your time, you must continue to act with great resolution. This is the time to take responsibility into your own hands, and to begin the light work.

Now that you have seen, studied, and learned, it is time to find the places where you will share your light. Do not be passive: volunteer in light organizations, volunteer in political parties and social organizations, wake up and make your voice heard. The power is in the hands of the people who are crying out for love, compassion, and peace.

Together with you, we are showering the area with the violet ray, the ray of transformation that will bring about mass awakening of dormant light beings. We are doing this in other parts of the world as well, but your area is the core of the globe; enter within your sacred heart and activate the violet ray every day to enlighten yourselves and those around you. Surrounding each one of you are many beings who are nourished by your energy, and the change you undergo will affect them as well. We are with you, marching hand in hand on the shared journey. Call us and we will envelop you in the love you so long for, the love that will speed up your work in the third dimension.

We are indeed on a unique path, and we of the city of Telos—the City of Light, are walking hand in hand with you light beings who have joined us through your heart and through your higher selves; you have joined us at the time we have chosen to meet in order to fulfill the promise of these marvelous, Messianic days, days of energetic change on the planet. In this period, human beings will begin to feel changes; some of you are already undergoing changes at the level of the physical, the etheric, and the emotional body. These changes will enable you to absorb the different vibrations of energy.

In this time, light work and growth are important as never before, and dormant light beings will be unable to continue the journey in the fifth dimension of Planet Earth. The current year on earth, 2013, is ending with grave changes to the planet; climatic, geological, and human changes will continue to occur globally and will become even more extreme. This is because Mother Earth is cleansing herself, and is, at the same time, receiving especially strong energies from the central sun. Solar flares are also having a strong effect on the planet. Soon, in your lifetime, you will witness volcanic eruptions resulting from global warming, which will continue in the coming decade. Many souls will leave the planet, and not only those living in what you call "the third world" will be affected, but natural disasters will strike many souls living in developed areas as well. We don't want to frighten you, and it's important for you to know that not all of humanity leaves the incarnation; however, you must understand that during this period, only those who connect to the vibrations of the heart and to their inner selves, will continue to exist.

Time is short. With the opening of the energetic portal on December 21, 2012, the Middle East began to undergo significant changes. Even several months beforehand, the region opened to the new frequency of the golden age. Leaders of the region are experiencing the vibrations sent by this frequency. The new energy will also influence the hearts of human beings, who will realize that only through harmony, giving, and understanding will they be able to continue to exist. Some will choose not to remain on the earth, but many others will make an essential change in the level of development of their souls and will continue on the path of light. Most souls in the region long for peace between the two peoples, the Ishmaelites and the Jews, and peace will indeed arrive. People of the region will be surprised to discover reserves of water in the desert that will help them survive.

You must realize the great importance of the peoples of this area. The Jews continue in their role, and begin to understand that they must accommodate the Arab peoples surrounding them. By the same token, the Arab peoples will accommodate the Jews and there will be reconciliation between them; however, this will happen only after a certain drama has played out in the region in your near future. The change is happening now and there can be no delay—this is the time to make decisions. Spread the light, spread the teaching, and continue to open the hearts of the population near you. Light beings have a purpose—each of you has taken on a role of healing or teaching, or has undertaken to become a master.

Dear ones, these are Messianic days, and it is time to awaken. Make decisions and go with your heart; think with your heart—the very place that has led you to the reading of this material, and the sacred place through which you are connected to the creator of the universe. Turn to your higher self, the pure place that you are now rejoining after hundreds of thousands of years of separation.

Beneath the pyramids at Luxor in Egypt, cities of light have existed for hundreds of thousands of years. When the children of Israel left slavery for freedom, the ancient Egyptians were given the job of spreading light work in their region, and so they did. But, after the destruction of the Second Temple, there began a period of darkness in the area, and it was very important to disseminate the light again. The light cities beneath the pyramids continued their work at a faster pace. In the light city of Luxor, we are already doing very significant work to maintain the Middle East. Many masters, kings, and light beings from all over the universe are arriving in the area to activate the light cities and spread their energy throughout the region, so that you can continue to exist there, despite the darkness, the many wars, the sorrow, and the pain.

Of course, there are also many light workers around the Red Sea, and the sensitive area of the Syria-African Rift is also receiving assistance. The area is being supported so that the energy given off by Mother Earth will not destroy the cities or exterminate the human beings living there. Additional work is being carried out in the Golan Heights, where many beings are drawn to perform light work beneath the surface for the healing of the area, which has known such great suffering. Healing is indeed taking place, and we call on you to join us to help. Join the energy centers as light groups and help Mother Earth to heal. This will bring about beneficial change more quickly.

With you, Adama.

Message from Master Sananda

Greetings dear ones, friends, and masters. I am Master Sananda, also known as Jesus Christ.

This region is my home, and here I have experienced many earthly incarnations. In the last of these, I was incarnated as Jesus. I came to this life in order to bring resurrection, to transmit and intensify the feeling of compassion, and by so doing to open the hearts of the masses—the entities who have come to earth into the third dimension. At a time when one people was being controlled by another, it was my intention to enlighten and empower the Jewish people who had been ruled by the Romans for a long time.

Indeed, with the help of many light entities, I was able to awaken the hearts of the population that lived in the region at the time, and human beings have since continued to sustain those vibrations. Sadly, there were also power and ego games being played among those entities. The ego of the dominant clergy of the time did not allow the idea of infinite compassion or love that came from the hearts of the masses. Their fear of losing control of the people, most of whom had faith in the Creator, made cooperation difficult and led to my downfall. Yet, through the ages, my spirit as Jesus in the Christian world has opened the hearts of many, and continues to do so to this day.

Message from Saint Germain[4]

At this time, I am revealed in the form of the renowned Master, Saint Germain. On my journeys, I pass all the points of light on earth, and many are connecting to the violet ray of transformation that surrounds the planet. We recently planted the ray in Jerusalem to initiate a significant change in human vibrations. This, together with the activation of the crystal, has indeed caused changes to begin. In order to continue on this path and make a greatly accelerated spiritual leap toward the light, you light workers must be diligent, and operate the crystal with vibrations of love.

Working with the violet ray is today more vital than ever. The ray has many qualities. It is composed of two rays, the blue and the pink, so that it comprises the energy of cosmic love, as well as the link to God's will. Using the ray intensifies and accelerates procedures and processes at various levels of vibration; hence, it should be generously used. At every point in your lives, when you encounter stagnation

---

[4] Master Saint Germain holds the position of Chohan of the Seventh Ray. He serves as the guardian of the violet flame of freedom and transformation for the planet.

or anger, send the ray to the condition or to the affected person and it will quickly free them and restore the proper flow of energy.

In our ceremonies at Telos, we use the ray for many purposes: the children amuse themselves with it; it helps clean and maintain the energetic bodies; and it accompanies us in moments of expansion. We invite you to the Temple of the Violet Flame, where the temple priests and I will guide you through the changes in vibration of your physical and etheric bodies. This will help and support you as you make a quantum leap onto the new path of enlightenment opening up in your lives.

Muster your courage; venture into your hearts and notice the lilac shade of violet of the sacred heart; continue to disseminate the violet ray into the deepest levels of your bodies, to the protons and electrons that build and operate the physical aspect, to the nerves and the cells; color your aura lilac and continue to work with the ray for seven days.

Change will take place with the speed that characterizes the spirit of the age. This is the time to enter the world of light, the world of truth that has been closed to you for such a long time; this is the time to open and connect to the light, the knowledge, and your higher self.

Call me and I will come.
Supporting you fully on your path,
Saint Germain.

The Gulf of Eilat—Meditation
I take a deep breath and enter a meditative state.

In my etheric body, I enter a chariot; the chariot hovers above the place where the Red Sea meets the Indian Ocean, then descends deep into the sea. The color is dark blue; dolphins accompany me to the depths.

Getting out of the chariot, I enter the inner space of a pyramid. In its center stands a dome-like structure made of crystal, around which light entities are seated. I understand that these are entities whose purpose it is to provide Mother Earth with vibrations of love and light, to help her purify the energy discharged from her depths, the energy that causes the movement of tectonic plates along the Syrian-African Rift.

In my etheric body, I sit down beside the dome located at the center of the pyramid. Inside it, I see the visible tip of the crystal, the body of which is buried deep in the earth. I stretch out my hands to the crystalline dome and feel the energy moving from my sacred heart toward the crystal. The crystal fills with glittering light; I feel its vibrations rising, and my body expands and fills with light. The light penetrates from the crystal deep into Mother Earth, and the whole Syrian-African Rift is bathed in shimmering light.

The light entities in the pyramid are tens of thousands of years old. Their assigned role is to guard the crystal pyramid that helps the compressed energies discharged by Mother Earth to be released in a gradual and controlled manner. I notice that during the healing, an energetic frequency passes among all the entities and joins them together.

The light entities explain to me that they enter and exit the pyramid, and that the pyramid is always manned in order to preserve the energetic balance in this fragile region of Mother Earth. They go on to clarify that there are additional places on the planet, temples of healing located in the depths of the seas and the oceans, which support the process of releasing energetic compression.

Surrounding the big pyramid stand small pyramids, connected to one another in a way that allows for charging of energies and individual treatment and support to the light beings that oversee the place.

After I bestow healing and experience, the healing that has occurred through my sacred heart, I thank the guide for having shared this knowledge with me. I take my leave telepathically, disengage from the pyramid, return to the chariot, and begin to rise.

Part II

Between Dimensions

The purpose of life in parallel dimensions is to help light entities learn and develop with greater speed.

New Times

Dear ones, you have indeed entered another transition in this period of earth's evolution. The earth is being showered with energy from the great central sun, in preparation for the arrival of the year 2014.

Dear ones, you are doing spiritual work, entering your sacred hearts, cleansing, completing lessons and karma, and opening up to the senses, to knowledge, and to incarnations in which you were masters, teachers, priests, and healers. The memories are returning; now is the time to bring back the knowledge and power and to meet with human beings, supporting those in need of healing, guiding them, and helping them absorb the new vibrations. The truth is coming to light; there is no room for secrets or drama; there is no room for the old energy. The ego no longer exists, and there is no longer room for lies and deceit; these days, power comes from the vibration of love, which is becoming more refined as it reenters people's hearts. People who work and live through the heart will be able to draw the truth to themselves, and they will create the new way. In contrast, humans who continue to act through the ego and create drama will preserve the old way and will live in darkness and fear of their reality.

We must therefore live in joy, observing as though through the eyes of a master, and cultivating a higher vibration. We must safeguard love, harmony, giving, and trust, and we must live truthfully. These are not cliches; this is the new energy, and only those who connect with it will be able to exist in the new dimension toward which Mother Earth is moving.

Dear humans, it is Kryon, Michael, the Council of Nine, and many light energies in the higher dimensions who are speaking with you. The energy of creation has been transmitting the knowledge for a long time, ever since the ancient times of the Maya, the ancient Egyptians, the people of Tibet, and many others. It is a time of change and rebirth; in the coming year, loved ones, all those who are not connected to their inner selves will have to awaken. These are not empty words; this is happening and this is the energy of truth. The present is here and now and there is no time to waste. We will soon hold another celebration for the long-awaited year. For about a month, we, in the light city of Telos, have been celebrating the entry of the new energy. We all take responsibility for the changes, and each of us fulfills his purpose.

We invite you to undergo healing in all the temples of the Seven Flames, to enter the sacred heart, our home, and connect to the knowledge of the crystals that fill each of the light cities on the planet. We invite you to the temples of healing and to the priestesses, in order to connect to the healing energy of our young people, the children of Telos.

Everything is accessible and everything is open. Connect to the fifth dimension, accept help from the Telos community available to you in your country—and support each other.

We send you the rays of love, compassion, trust, and giving. Remember that we are with you, strengthening, and supporting you. We are aware of your strong yearning for home; we fortify and support you. We will meet soon, brothers and sisters. Remember your choice on earth.

Passage between the Dimensions

I am happy to continue guiding you and transmitting the knowledge that is now passing from us in the fifth dimension to you dear humans living in the third dimension. The passage between the dimensions changes the energetic balance of your physical bodies, and you must know how to recalibrate the energy so that you can maintain yourselves at the higher frequencies. We are witness to all the changes in your spiritual development and are leading you, hand in hand, step by step, as you would guide with love and support a small child entering his new delicate body in the first year of his life.

You must understand that each of you is an immense light entity; it is difficult to describe in words the size of your energetic body. You are living in a number of parallel dimensions, and you are not just the human body with which you are familiar. The purpose of living in parallel dimensions is to help the light entity learn and develop more rapidly; because your soul has chosen many lessons and many experiences, you must aspire to reach the day when you will complete the lessons and be reunited with an enlightened and powerful light body in which you can continue to evolve. Of course, the new reality will be different because the third dimension will cease to exist for you; you are in the midst of a process, and for this process patience, understanding, and inner listening to your sacred heart are required.

Dear ones, we are witness to the changes many sons of light are making at this time; you are awakening to the Lemurian call and leaving behind the old and familiar patterns, whose energy no longer suits you and no longer serves you. Because the vibrations of this energy are low, you feel the need to leave your place of work, or even friends who were once close to you—you cannot continue to be in their company due to the changes you are undergoing. You must get used to the new reality and the new energy, and learn to live in these circumstances in which both the old and new energies exist at the same time. We are not telling you to leave all that is familiar, but begin adapting to parallel lives—the old and the new. You are advancing rapidly and there will soon be a separation between the new world and the old. You will lead the new energies, the new fifth dimension created on Mother Earth. Therefore, dear ones, continue to cleanse your bodies at all three levels—the emotional, the physical, and the spiritual.

It is not simple to do this work alone, and so join in with the light communities to which you are attracted. The Telos Israel community is one of them, and those who join it come from a very ancient place, a place revealed to you recently: ancient Lemuria, your home. The memories arise because the home is found within you. This doesn't mean you will be leaving soon—not at all, the opposite is true. You have chosen to lead humanity and your own awakening is part of this process; you will assist those who follow your lead in moving forward.

Dear ones, remember your home—cry, laugh, write down your memories—now is the time. Know that you have a very important role in the process of change now taking place on the planet, and we are with you. Of course, your souls continue to visit us in Telos. You meet with your families from ancient Lemuria, sometimes consciously and sometimes during sleep. You must understand that we support you with great love and you are not alone. Be aware of that. We embrace you and empower you each and every moment; have complete faith and continue your light work confidently; maintain proper nutrition; enter our temples, and practice meditation.

Energetic Gateways

Dear ones, at this time the meetings you hold have great importance. On every date that is an energetic gateway, the heavens open and a certain amount of energy enters the surface and is absorbed into Mother Earth. Your role, light entities, is to anchor the energies so they will be absorbed into the earth in a balanced way. Your bodies, which have undergone significant changes recently and have been reborn, will help anchor the energies and bring about change, so that the planet will continue to raise its vibration. Humans who reach the days of light expansion will experience an important phase in their spiritual development.

Surrounding Planet Earth there exists an extremely delicate web of crystals. This web is connected through a fine network to the crystals planted in the earth, which are returning to activity after a long dormant period. Your DNA is changing; it is expanding, awakening, and opening to the codes hidden within it. As the crystal network connects with the DNA in the human body, the DNA helices will begin to vibrate. Thus, humanity will reconnect to the knowledge of the light code that was granted to you many ages ago by the original light entities who first landed on the planet. The period during which these seeds were first planted is when the Creator decided to establish a star on which there would be personal, exclusive choice for each soul that arrived. The original intention was to establish a world that would live in love, harmony, and communion, allowing the soul to create and fulfill its potential to the highest level. As we know, however, things turned out differently.

Today we are reconnecting with the crystals. You are the pioneers and the leaders. This is why your role is so important.

The Gateway of November 11, 2011

The gateway of November 11, 2011 (11.11.11) was a powerful gateway, through which entities of light, vibrating at the right frequency, can continue their march on the path of light.

Dear ones, at this time, with the changes the planet is undergoing and with the changes your physical bodies are about to experience, you must make your own choices. Not everyone will experience the change; many human beings will continue to live in the third dimension, in the drama, anger, lack of awareness and disconnection from their divine spark. However, much of humanity is awakening and remembering the life familiar to them from the age of Lemuria, from the age of the gods, when we all walked on the continent, and through choice, love, and harmony created the reality of paradise.

Indeed, we all remember those days. That memory is embedded in the intrinsic codes of your physical body and in our heavenly light bodies. Thus, we are all marching in the path of light, marching again for harmony and for the vibrations of love. Dear ones, these are Messianic days.

We in Telos are in connection with the supreme council and are acting with the masters, angels, and eminent light entities who have chosen at this time to be in active cooperation with us and with you, human beings, in order to awaken your dormant hearts once again. This time is the most important in the divine game, the game that gives us the ability to choose; indeed, Mother Earth has chosen, and human beings have chosen—we are awakening!

You must understand, dear ones, the great gateway that opened on November 11, 2011, was essential to the cosmic gateway opening of 2012. Many of the light entities transmitting messages through you, human beings, speak of this gateway; this is the doorway for particles of life from the central sun. These particles are filtered and then assimilated into your bodies to awaken the particles of life in your crystal bodies. Your crystal bodies will join heart to heart, and together will ignite the network of crystals surrounding the planet. That crystal network will join the magnetic grid to support future exchanges of codes. In this way, the planet will become stable.

The crystal network plays a most important role in the permanent linking of the planet to the higher dimensions. This union will be complete when this network and the sons of light are reunited.

Dear ones, you are awakening in your multitudes, and you are experiencing that feeling which returns you home; you are opening to the light, opening to loved ones around you, and to light entities from other dimensions. You understand that what surrounds you is alive and well. Even if it is not always comprehensible to you and even if it is not visible to the human eye, what surrounds you is happening; it is expanding and changing, and undergoing ascension to the fifth dimension.

With the opening of this important gateway, you are witnessing many changes. Those leaders who represent the old energies, which can no longer exist on the planet, are falling from power and disappearing, as are all those who cannot contain the light vibrations that are entering Planet Earth. Thus, the darkest corners are revealed to the sons of light, and the light finds its way to the hearts of awakening human beings. Changes will continue to occur. Old organizations in which the darkness still exists, will continue to play out their part, but the light will spread into all the places that can exist only in the fifth dimension.

The planet is undergoing changes; Mother Earth, in her benevolence, protects human beings; she absorbs the chaos and the pollution. With the help of aliens arriving from distant universes, the cleansing is being done. The cleansing needs your empowerment; dear humans who are opening your hearts, this is your time to protect the rain forests, the oceans, and the seas; this is your time to protect the coasts and the last areas of land still free of and pavement preferred by the forces of control and darkness. This is your time to wake up, to march and to say what is in your heart; find the inner light, take action that makes room for enlightenment and protect our home, the blue star. At this time, dear ones, you must penetrate the golden flame that is suffusing the planet, and take full responsibility for the change that is occurring.

We are with you, whispering to you at night when your etheric body is on its way to Telos and other cities of light; we guide you and show you the possibilities open before you at this time; we are with you, supporting your body that is weary of exploitation, darkness, and imbalance. You are awakening and your children are crying out for change; your children, who do not remember the source of nature or the powers of light, but are captives of the restrictive energies of control. You must awaken and leave the lethargy that has taken control of you through computers and television. Wake up from the spell that controls your culture and closes your heart; it is time for the awakening, time to hear the whisperings of nature and of the animals barely surviving on the planet; it is time to go out, to listen, and to shout out your inner cry that has been suppressed for tens of thousands of years.

Dear ones, we are with you, accompanying you and hearing you, and together with you, we are accomplishing the change.

"Hallelujah!" we must shout, "The awakening is happening. Hallelujah!"

We see the sons of light fighting to preserve the last bits of earth's undisturbed surface. Those same sons of light are rising up to bring about change; they are leaving behind the familiar, the material, and the compliant conduct; they are turning back to the original path of awakening, of free choice, of concern for the planet, and leading humanity into the fifth dimension.

"Big Brother"

Good evening and welcome. This is Adama, the High Priest of Telos, welcoming all our dear readers, the light entities who are opening their hearts to the Lemurian vibration in these Messianic days.

The changes are indeed rapid, the cleansing is deep and powerful, and Mother Earth is acting according to ancient memories. Lemuria and Atlantis are examples of changes that occurred in the past; the continent of Lemuria plunged into the depths when Mother Earth carried out a cleansing, and the result was a change occurred in the vibration of the globe.

The decision to carry out a significant change in the manner of learning on the planet came from the highest source; in cooperation with the Council of Nine, with our brothers from the Pleiades and with the masters, it was decided to conduct a game in which light entities would descend to earth and attempt, without a direct connection to their divinity, to plant the seeds of humanity on the planet. So it was, and so the human race was created. Although the creation is identical to the etheric-energetic structure of the sons of Lemuria, this connection was severed and humanity walked step by step on its path to reconnect with the divine source.

Today, dear ones, many are awakening to the inner call arriving again from a high source; hearts are opening, DNA is changing, and a great deal of knowledge is flowing to the surface. You, dear ones, are waking human beings and teaching them. We invite you to make a change at this time, to take responsibility and spread the knowledge. Understand that most of the knowledge is accessible to all and it is the right of every human being to connect and learn.

Dear ones, understand that you are working and performing your mission in cooperation with higher energies, and together you will enlighten the planet. Take note of how you feel when you connect with us in the fifth dimension, and then when you descend again to the human level in the third dimension. Speak the language of the heart and bring the high vibration back with you to the third dimension. Support one another with love.

We in Telos look into the crystal screens and see you playing the game of "Big Brother." Do you think it is accidental that this game is being televised at this particular time? No, it is no accident. The energetic change on the earth is broadcast to the entire universe, and the eyes of all, in this and parallel universes, are upon you because you are at the center.

The angle of earth's ecliptic plane has changed, and its location relative to the sun will also change. This alteration to the celestial map is essential in order for soft energies to enter the globe, and enables them in the fifth dimension. Not all human beings will make a change; those who do not make the change will continue their lessons on those stars where the third dimension continues to exist.

The light cities will open to the sons of light and the contact between us will increase. Not everyone will be present at these meetings; only those light entities whose physical and etheric bodies can withstand our energies will attend—so eat properly, drink water, do lots of sports, and breathe deeply.

We are sending healing energy to the Middle East, which is undergoing a considerable energetic change at this time. Be patient, because the truth will be known; the forces of light are occupying the energetic space and change will come. In the near future, a new leader will come to the Jews. This is a leader who has led the Kingdom of Israel in the past, and will return this time in a new incarnation. The Jewish nation is close to achieving its mission and will complete its karma. Prepare for the coming of the Messiah. This is a true prophecy; you need only be patient and recall that your time is different from our time. Dear ones, as you see, many changes are about to occur. Continue your mission and perform your light work with faith. We invite you to the light city of Telos, to partake of its healing energies to strengthen, build, and balance yourselves.

Survey of Reality

Welcome, this is Adama, the High Priest of Telos, blessing the special day on which additional knowledge is disseminated to the inhabitants of Planet Earth.

We are here in the Council building, in the meeting room, seated before the crystal table, where we have been working for some time with the inhabitants on the surface. Until recently we transmitted messages through a few human light entities, but at present there is a mass awakening, particularly in the Middle East region, in Eretz Yisrael, and we are sharing more knowledge.

Lemurian entities have arrived for their significant incarnation; they are connecting to the sacred heart, to the memory of distant times when they were forced to leave their homes in ancient Lemuria, the immense continent where they led a different life, one of harmony and love. Most of you held various positions at the time, but we all felt from the heart, and we all received our powers from the Creator—from the source of light, without ego, without judgment or competition or various other low-frequency characteristics. The brain existed, but it was smaller and operated differently; its two structures worked in a balanced way. The subconscious was accessible and open, and thought was not linear as it is today; rather, it existed at all levels and on all planes.

The heart is the place that connects with the essence of your soul, and most of you have not yet experienced the emotion of love from this place. Today we, the Seven Masters of the Seven Flames, are here with you, along with many members of our Telosian family: Aurelia Louise Jones, who has returned home to the essence of her soul, with Anahamar, with our dear Zohar, with representatives of our priesthood, one of "The Pink Brotherhood," and many of our children and animals and plants. We are with you, ready to transmit an important message to humanity.

What is the vibration of love? Is it possible to understand what love is? Your scientists have been studying it for hundreds of years, trying to "quantify" the emotion that is so important in your world. The vibration of love is a source of light and energy that comes from the Creator who created us all. This energy is the beginning of life, a vibration with which we can create. In Lemuria, we lived from this place, and in your world, too, life is created through love; however, in recent human history, this vibration has waned.

We are happy to inform you that at present you are again connecting with the vibration of love. Take care to speak and think through the heart. Avoid drama. Heal yourselves via the heart. When you carry out light activity, you are healing Mother Earth and charging her crystals; you are creating harmony through the heart. So enter your heart and love yourselves. Your light entity exists not only within your physical body, but also beyond it. Therefore, when you connect with the heart in the present, it influences your entire light entity.

Your ego has many aspects, including those in parallel lives, so that when you heal one heart, the hearts of all your other parallel aspects are healed as well. The crystal network that functions as the basis of the planet works through energy, and the same is true of flora and fauna. Take care to live your daily lives from a place of love. If you have a bad day, listen to music that opens the heart chakra; if you have a fight or bring painful energy into your heart, perform immediate healing. The vibrations are working now at a fast tempo and your light bodies, which you have healed in recent meetings with us, are very sensitive. Protect yourself when you go out into the world or when you encounter the third dimension, and take care when you encounter bodies that carry a vibration different from your own. Your vibrations are very delicate and such contact is liable to lower them. Remember that your family members are influenced by you, so it is important that you interact with them, particularly with your children.

Daily cleansing is essential; use the flames we work with in Telos; at this time, they are refining and assisting life in the third dimension. Be sure to eat properly and drink plenty of water. Attend group meetings that are uplifting for you. There is support through light work, which is actually a different language and a different reality. As we sit here with you in the council meeting, we see how the wonderful light entities on the surface of the earth take their mission seriously and are working diligently to change the vibrations and to change reality on your planet. We bless you for your deeds and for your daring.

Earth is changing and you are witnessing the change in the day-to-day reality of the Middle East. There are many light groups and each has a role; your role is to help change the situation. Indeed, the light entities are fighting against darkness, and this time, dear ones, the light is especially strong. The earth has not been as enlightened as it is now in these Messianic days; the light fills the hearts of the sons of light, and you are the sons of light. Today there is chaos in some countries in the Middle East, but it will be followed by harmony; this will happen in your lifetime. Be patient.

The change is also occurring in other parts of the world, and those places are experiencing a healing process. The African continent is undergoing a significant change, and it will become stronger and continue to ascend. The cleansing there has been happening for close to thirty years and is nearing completion. The countries that have exploited Africa will begin to correct this karma and will invest capital in developing the continent and channeling its resources for the good of the local people. The continent of Asia will reach a balanced population through the choice of the people. America will return to simplicity and cleanliness, and purge itself of corruption.

Thus, the globe will find balance.

Therefore, dear ones, continue the light work. Connect with light groups that are active and taking the initiative; join them and exert an influence. That is the only way to continue the process. We are working in cooperation with you and need you just as you need us, because together we are the whole.

    We love you and are with you,

    Adama and the other family members

Japan

A message that arrived following the tsunami in Japan.

At present, the region of the Japanese islands in the Pacific Ocean is undergoing a strong energetic purification, and you are witnessing the changes that Mother Earth is experiencing. At this time you, too, are undergoing evolutionary changes. Your DNA is expanding; the additional helices are working. Your emotional-mental body is opening and discovering additional levels, and in the present incarnation, your inner eyes are discovering the connection to the divine source and the knowledge linked to the choice of your personal contract. With this new knowledge, you understand that the changes are happening first and foremost to Mother Earth. For this to happen to you and Mother Earth simultaneously, there must be a connection between you and the planet. This is the reason for the extreme events that are taking place. Although the release of compressed energy takes place rapidly, in this way you correct yourselves efficiently and undergo rapid inner cleansing.

At this time, karma is being cleared and you feel heaviness and fatigue from the old pains that are arising. You must also be sensitive and know that in the coming decade you will return to balance with the physical and emotional bodies.

If you are to be able to connect with the fifth dimension and live in it at any given moment, the balance must be perfect. The physical body and the emotional body must be united because there is no room for the disharmony so common in your world. You must connect with the divine will through the vision of the masters; for most of you, the present incarnation is the last, hence many of you can observe life through the eyes of a master.

At present, many light workers are opening to their deepest levels, their vision is clearing, responsibility is intensifying, and activity is flowering. From within these energies, we are working with you. With some of you, we are establishing personal ties in order to spread positive vibrations to all of humanity in the third dimension.

You must understand, dear ones, that we in Telos in Mt. Shasta, observe you and meet with you on a daily basis with the intention of strengthening and empowering your souls. The longing for home often arises from your daily visits in our temples and meetings with loved ones. When you are in a state of wakefulness, the higher soul yearns, while the partial awareness that is in the physical body does not know why. Hence, you leave and return.

Dear ones, know that we are with you even when your senses are not aware of our presence. Continue cleansing your body; in the monthly meetings with groups of the Telos community, you can perform cleansing that will stay with you for thirty days. The continuous work with light is important—just as your physical fitness declines if you don't train, so too the vibrations quickly drop if they are unattended for a few days. We therefore insist on monthly meetings with you.

In the course of the changes that are taking place in the world, certain locations will rise to the surface, and others on the planet will disappear. In many places, events will take place that will change history as you know it. This process, which will take place in the coming decade, will change life on the entire planet.

We ask that you continue with the work of disseminating the light that you perform so faithfully. We invite you to come en masse to Mt. Shasta and visit us in the light city of Telos, for spiritual empowerment and ongoing-shared work in order to intensify the vibrations on the globe. We join with you on your personal journey; we support and accompany you. The memories are returning and the promises are revealed again; Lemuria calls you home. Indeed, it is time to return.

Bless you,
With you, Adama

Part III

Telos

In creating Telos, we created an existence shared by all the beings who survived the sinking of the continent of Lemuria. The bonds among us and our coming together for a common purpose are what made us a unified force and led us to create the light city Telos.

A Visit to the Light City Telos

Welcome, I am Adama.

Telos is one of the most beautiful light cities on the planet. The city exists as a self-sustaining community, and is responsible for safeguarding the fifth dimension. The residences and temples were built accordingly: the healing temples and residences of the people of Telos are creations of thought from the heart, in ongoing communion with the creator.

Dear ones, when you wish to create your reality, you must know how to look inward to your heart; the first divine spark of creation is that which awakens the inner diamond within you, the same diamond that encourages you to act. Action, therefore, shapes your being and propels the universe into creation. A powerful feeling from the heart must accompany the intention of the thought; when this happens, creation begins.

When we were creating Telos, we created an existence shared by all the beings who were saved from the sinking of the continent of Lemuria. Our connection to one another and our devotion to the shared goal are what generated the solidarity, allowing us to create the light city Telos through the expression of intention. The particles of creation are filled with the frequency of the flame of resurrection, which is the frequency of creation and action, awakening and renewal. The light city Telos is still being built and undergoing changes to this day.

The Buildings in Telos

Most of the healing temples in Telos are built in the shape of a pyramid. The pyramid is the correct geometrical form for healing because it contains and preserves the frequency that is developed in the course of the healing work. The ray of creation enters through the center of the pyramid, connecting with and strengthening its flame, and the structure preserves the energetic centering that is developed during the healing.

The structures in Telos are made of crystal. Crystal is a material that can intensify the frequency more than a hundredfold, and in this way, what you receive is greatly amplified. Furthermore, the shape of the base of the pyramid allows for fixation; when the energy at the base is fixed and unchanging, the healing continues at the frequency appropriate for the patient being treated.

The dwellings in Telos are round crystal structures that create a frequency of inclusion. Unlike a quadrilateral building, the rounded building prevents the accumulation of compressed energy. In your houses, energy is often compressed into the corners, causing a lack of natural flow that is so vital to the balance of the bodies living in the structure. In the round structure, on the other hand, the flow creates continuity of the sensory process you experience during the day.

In the central plaza of Telos, burns the city's flame, the flame of ascension, the white flame that has burned constantly for tens of thousands of years, and is never extinguished.

The flame balances the frequencies of the beings who are in motion and in action; during the day it sends its rays to any being who loses balance. The flame senses what we are experiencing so there is no need to stop in order to connect with it. It sends its rays great distances outside the solar system and the universe as well. The bond between the people of the light city Telos and the flame has existed since the very beginning of the city. Indeed, this flame was the first to come into being with the creation of the city.

The choice of the people of the light city Telos was to go out and join human beings; we realized that this was the only way we could transmit and speed up the distribution of the light and distribution of the frequency of love. Dear ones, for hundreds of thousands of years we lived in the light city secretly, with no link to most human beings. In the course of history, there were those who came to us and chose to stay, and others who met us and took the light with them; they guarded the mountain from anyone whose soul was unclean and was not yet ready to be exposed.

The mountain is a sacred place that constitutes a main energy center. Energy from the central sun reaches it, and is distributed throughout the planet. The mountain is a central energetic portal to which light entities arrive from all over the galaxy. It is not the only central point of light; other portals exist on the planet, but at present, the mountain is the central active portal. Most extraterrestrials arrive through it. Until now, entering and leaving the mountain was done in secret, but today more and more human beings are becoming aware of the possibility of passing between dimensions. They are sensitive to the strong energies and vibrations surrounding the mountain, and communicate with our friends from other planets. The time of disclosure is nearing. The government of the state where the mountain is located is aware of what is happening, and is acting in cooperation with the activity in the mountain.

Our role is to guarantee the continued dissemination of the light that enters the mountain. Therefore, the extraterrestrial friends who arrive are acting on behalf of the light and carry out missions to accelerate enlightenment on Planet Earth. It is also our job to enlighten human beings, and in the exciting cooperation with you, we are carrying out the enlightenment step by step. There is a certain percentage of humans who are aware of our existence, but as I said, not all have awakened. Among humans who are awakening, there are those who connect with their extraterrestrial brothers, those who connect with sons of light who have arrived from various past civilizations, and those who connect with their Lemurian heart.

You, dear ones, sons of the Jewish people, have arrived and connected with the people of Telos. Your hearts have opened to the light coming from our hearts as it expands. Many Lemurian souls have chosen to come into the very heart of the Jewish people in order to help them through the stages of sacred resurrection that are taking place at this time in the light city Jerusalem; there exists a close connection between the Jewish people and the Lemurians. Although the energies are different—the energy of the Jewish people is masculine energy, while the Lemurians express feminine energy—the source is the same. You must understand that creation and generation are of God, the only creator and source of the energies for Jews and Lemurians; they share a common purpose as well: to spread the light. Return to the Jewish scriptures, to the sources that speak of spreading the light through the heart, and realize that the source is identical.

Dear ones, many Lemurians are scattered across the planet. The central light city is in Telos in Mt. Shasta, but you must realize that we have agreed to be dispersed by choice, in order to bring light to those places that are in darkness. At this time, there is a mass awakening and we are happy about it. We see you meeting and working in the name of the light, and we are witness to the personal healing you are undergoing and the planetary healing you are performing.

We respect you for this and thank you. Through this exciting cooperation, we can continue toward the goal of enlightening the planet. The change is already happening and it will continue to grow through 2012. Throughout this year, it will be possible to choose to awaken. The face of Mother Earth is changing and human beings are choosing the light. You are witnessing the era prophesied by the wise men of various religious. This is a sacred era. Be blessed in your work. I caress you with the rays of love that come from our temples; I bless you with healing rays and support you, joining with you in every moment.

Adama

The Upper Light Cities

The light city Telos observes you, dear ones, and many other light cities on the planet see the sons of light applying themselves to the matter of ascension and the divine plan. Many changes are taking place in the light cities and the joy is great. You must understand that in the light cities we have been preparing for the present era. Many cities that exist in the depths of the earth are choosing at this time, with precise and careful planning, only those regions that contain the frequencies of the fifth dimension, regions where the electrons and protons can operate to their full potential and in their full resonance.

New light cities are being built as upper cities. At this time, heavenly Jerusalem is being built; the third temple too is being built, and it will be open to those sons of light whose etheric bodies can withstand the vibrations and enter its complex. Above Tibet, another light city is being built; it will help free Tibet from the Chinese. Above Egypt, a light city is being built that will help open the portal for extraterrestrials who have entered through that portal in the past. In the light city Telos, we are preparing to build a light city above

Mt. Shasta in the United States; this light city will heal the entire American continent. As the vibrations increase, the region will attract many sons of light from Planet Earth and throughout the universe.

We in Telos have set up new teams for this purpose, and are building the upper light city for Mt. Shasta. When the time comes, we will invite you to observe what is being done. Indeed, dear ones, we are joyful at the mass awakening of the sons of light. We bless all who come to Mt. Shasta and choose, in full awareness, to join the mission of Telos, who choose to spread anew the Lemurian light vibrations, and who choose to reawaken to the codes and the wisdom of the divinity within you.

This is the time to unite; these are Messianic days. We observe you and read what you feel in your heart; we are aware of your struggle with the karma that is being resolved at this time.

Be aware of the changes, raise the vibrations of your bodies through your consciousness; work and act in teams, as we are doing in Telos; act from your heart, with a sense of mission, and give to the community in which you live. Act from a pure place, without judging, without competitiveness, and without ego or exploitation. Those are conditions whose time is past.

We and your families are with you day and night, accompanying you through every ancient memory that arises, and healing you at all the deep levels. You are beautiful sons of light, you are enchanting sons of light, you are sons of light who have chosen to awaken and ascend. Continue spreading more and more. Understand that the transformation is happening. At first, you will not be completely aware of it, but little by little, the transformation will permeate throughout your lives.

Sons of light make up a critical mass; you will feel the change through revolutions and significant events that have a public impact; you will feel the change in your close family and in people who are near you; you will feel the change in your hearts. Those who choose not to change will have to deal with challenges that lead them to make a new choice.

Indeed, dear ones, these are the days. We in Telos see you, extend our hands to you, and support you.

Telos City Council

A Journey of Healing to the Light City Luxor

We take a deep breath and fill our bodies with a sparkling white ray of light. We are seated in a carriage, in a circle full of sparkling light, and the carriage begins to rise. It rises into the atmosphere, and with the speed of light arrives at the pyramid of Giza. We enter a beam of sparkling white light that takes us deep into the pyramid, and we continue down into the belly of the earth, to the light city Luxor. Adama, the High Priest, accompanies us during the process and tells us about the city.

The light city Luxor was established after the sinking of Lemuria. The sons of light who arrived and built the light city, built the pyramids that became an energetic center for millions of years. The center constituted a main entry portal for extraterrestrials who came to continue sowing the seeds for the development of humanity. The frequency of the sons of light who settled in Luxor at the time of its founding was higher than that of the humans on the surface of the land, and the city became a light center for the entire Middle East. The light entities that lived in Luxor, and live there to this day, constitute an important energetic center on the planet.

During certain periods, the sons of light who lived on the surface of the land had links with some of the light beings of the light city Luxor and could enter the city by raising the vibration of their body to that of the fifth dimension. But this situation ended when the level of human consciousness dropped, and Luxor, which had been known as a center of ascension and initiation, became a place where, for tens of thousands of years, few entered its temples.

Today, with the opening of the portals and the rise of the sons of light among humanity, beings who once lived in the light city are finding their way back and are connecting anew to the light frequency in the temples of Luxor. Luxor is linked with all the light cities that are connected to the central sun center on the planet. The light entities in Luxor came there from the star Sirius. The temple of ascension of Master Serapis Bey is located in Luxor, a temple bearing the flame of ascension—the flame that penetrates the hearts of those sons of light who are changing. The flame of ascension is responsible for the opening of the chakra centers, the connection with the "I Am," and the connection with the frequency of ascension. During the years when human consciousness was in decline, light beings continued to exist. The last master to enter and leave the light city was Thoth, who held a key to the transformation of consciousness.

The role of light beings in Luxor is, first of all, to purify the atmosphere of the planet. Without purification and an increase in oxygen, humanity would already have become extinct, because the number of humans living on Mother Earth is too large relative to the natural sources of oxygen available. The light city, therefore, carries out, day and night, activities of recharging and expanding the available energy. The community that lives in the city temples of healing is small but active. Unlike the community in Telos, the community in Luxor is not expanding because the birthrate is controlled. Every soul that enters the light city is assigned a specific role, and life is carefully planned.

Most of the sons of light in Luxor are tens of thousands of years old, and each entity has a significant, multi-faceted role that demands skill. At this time, the energetic frequency in the vicinity of Luxor—Egypt and neighboring countries—is undergoing great change, and the city is assisting in that process. Beginning in 2010, the violet flame has begun to emerge from the vortex of the pyramid almost every day, and baths the entire region.

Our carriage stops at the center of the healing level and we get out. We see before us a tall guide who welcomes us and asks us to follow him. We look at the walls of the city, the paintings of the ancients, the inscriptions in ancient Egyptian writing, hieroglyphics and another unfamiliar script, characteristic of the writing of the people of the city. We walk to a very large pyramid-shaped room and are asked to stand at the center. The room is made of opaque stone composed of crystal and various metals. In the center of the room is a gigantic golden crystal ball. We notice that within it there are air bubbles. These are bubbles formed by gases in the depths of the earth. They penetrate the crystal where they undergo a change and become oxygen bubbles. The crystal releases them, through an energetic opening out into the atmosphere. In Luxor, there are many such crystal balls in operation at any given moment.

Continuing behind the guide, we reach a healing level. In front of us stand crystal chairs; we sit down on them facing toward a wall made of gold. Let us contemplate the color, extend our hands to the golden wall, and feel the frequency of the gold entering our bodies. The frequency is powerful; this gold is a metal that has undergone alchemy; it is pure and clean. We can see that at this very moment golden rays emerge from the wall to the center of our sacred heart; the heart is charged with a high frequency that accelerates the flow of electrons and protons in our bodies. The ray encourages us to feel the frequency of truth, the frequency that opens the closed places in the heart, places flooded with feelings and experiences from the present and other incarnations; the truth is bathed in the golden ray, and we begin to feel the energetic release of the frequency that had been repressed. Perhaps an event from the distant past is beginning to dissolve and be released from the heart.

This powerful flame penetrates every feeling that has been repressed; as they are freed, the energy dissolves and disappears. We see our heart cleansed, and if there remains a part of our body that needs energetic cleaning, this is the time to dissolve it and release it from the heart chakra. Now we breathe deeply; we feel the center of our sacred heart expanding and a golden color illuminating it. With the next breath, our body grows wider and longer; we are invited to see the rays of the flame being spread throughout our bodies.

The High Priest Adama and other priests from Luxor stand facing us, and send golden rays of light toward us that encompass our entire being. All our bodies are bathed in the gentle flame that charges them with the frequency of expansion and growth. Now we take leave of the crystal chairs, thank the golden wall and everyone who was present with us, and accompanied by the guide from Luxor, we return to the carriage and sit down inside. The carriage closes and begins to operate, returning to the Land of Israel, to the room from which we set out.

We breathe deeply and reconnect with our physical body.

The Process of Emerging from the Mountain

Greetings, this is Adama.

In these times, dear ones, humanity is undergoing the long-awaited process of emerging from the darkness into the light. We of Telos in the fifth dimension, are observing you and witnessing all the changes and knowledge coming to you from light entities. You must understand that the sons of light in the light city are very active. They hold key positions in preparation for the next stage for humanity, the stage of awakening. In this phase, you will have the ability to raise the vibration of your physical bodies and be aware of all your human aspects. When the percentage of light energy is high enough, we will be able to emerge from our light cities and integrate into your social and community life.

Our integration among you is a challenging mission in which only a few sons of light are interested in taking part. Understand that when we leave the fifth dimension, we cannot return to it and we must remain in the third dimension in all its density. This is why, at this time, only a few sons of light are interested in coming out to the surface; however, we are aware that in the coming decade, this will change. In the town of Mt. Shasta in the United States, there are already some ten volunteers who are willing to emerge, in the near future, onto the surface in order to accelerate the spread of enlightenment from the mountain to open Lemurian hearts. Mt. Shasta is a most central portal. It will continue to attract many sons of light from across the planet and from other universes. There are a number of secret tunnels that lead to certain places in the mountain and are energetic portals in and out of it. We in the light city respect the guardians of the mountain and are grateful to our friends who guard the entrances and the exits.

Dear ones, we in the light city await your visits with us. We wait for you to come to treat your light bodies and open up to the knowledge passing between your energy centers—those chakras that open and are exposed again to the ancient knowledge. We are working in cooperation with you for the purpose of disseminating the light.

We understand the strong desire to be exposed to spiritual knowledge. Realize that the time has been chosen carefully and the awakening of human beings is an orderly process. We do not wish to cause alarm; therefore, we are transmitting the knowledge in accordance with humanity's level of preparedness to receive the light teachings. In the coming fifty years, however, the passage between the light cities on the planet will be rapid and intense; the picture will become clear and more and more cities will be open to visits by sons of light during their meditations.

Friends from Another Star

Welcome, dear ones. This is an exciting day in Telos. You are connected to the Lemurian heart; you have been here before in a different era when we were one, and now we are rejoining our strengths and our lights. The awakening is global, occurring all over the planet. Many Lemurians are awakening on every continent, each in his own time and within his own knowledge. Many Lemurian souls have chosen to be incarnated in your region. The Telos community has grown in a short time; it is already large and will continue to grow and become more powerful. Many Lemurians have chosen particularly harsh lessons, particularly in the region of the Middle East, a region saturated with hatred, wars, and bloodshed.

This current era will be different; this will be an era of love, harmony, and compassion. When we come and whisper in your ears, we awaken you to these days of joy; hence when this energy calls you, your heart awakens. Each and every one of you present, has a significant role related to the continued spreading of the light and raising of the vibrations for all of Planet Earth. As you know, the planet is undergoing change, in the wake of which human hearts will awaken (although not all of them), and will help Mother Earth pass to a new time. The next era will be very different from the current one with which she struggles in these days of rebirth.

Within the framework of change, the poles are shifting and the weather is transforming. Volcanoes are erupting and cleaning out the pollution, that to our great regret, you human beings have inflicted on the earth in such a short time. Human beings around the world will have to go through difficult days, and some will knowingly choose to leave the planet. The planet is moving to a new place, a new dimension, and in the passage from old to new, there will be new circumstances to deal with. Many light entities have spoken about this subject in recent years; the great entity Kryon's transmissions began in 1987.

These are Messianic days and our role is to disseminate light through the vibration of love. This vibration will open hearts, enabling us to awaken as many human beings as possible who choose to remain on the planet and continue sustaining humanity. Humanity has a most important role; human beings have worked very hard to reach this moment, and we want them to stay on the planet. The immense energy you call "the Creator" is aware of your choice; indeed, the freedom of choice between awakening and remaining asleep is real.

Our role, by virtue of the commitment we have taken upon ourselves, is to help human beings, as have the Pleiadians and many other friends from other stars. You, dear ones, are here today to spread the light. Do it in your spare time, among your family, friends, and especially, in the land of Israel.

The Telos Israel community has a specific task: to disseminate the light and encourage awakening in the Middle East so that the light from Israel will expand out to enlighten the Arab peoples. The Arab peoples will have an awakening as well, and highly significant global changes will take place in the Middle East, changes that will bring peace and harmony. We will reach for a fifth dimensional vibration of love and harmony. This may sound utopian to you, but it is not; we are witness to your yearning for renewal and acknowledge the challenging path you are struggling to traverse at this time. The new is indeed coming, but you must remember that your surroundings still resonate with the old vibration. We therefore recommend that you purify your bodies so they can absorb the energy transitions. Meditate every morning for about ten minutes so that you can come to us in a conscious way and perform purification in the healing temples of Telos. If you do this, you will be able to get through your day in the third dimension more easily.

It is very important for you to be in balance. If you lose your balance, stop and count to three; take a new breath and recharge the energy in your bodies. You must be clean so that you can more easily transmit the energies to the human beings around you. Live through the heart. Dear ones, pay attention to the choices you make. Avoid addiction to things that reduce your vibrations—places, foods, or habits. Low vibrations prevent you from doing light work and rising to the fifth dimension; they interfere with your fulfilling the mission to which you are committed, the Lemurian mission: disseminating the vibration of love and returning to ancient times when you were great masters and lived in harmony. In those days, your energy was not trapped in your physical body; you were able to contain enormous energy and realize your dreams and your purpose without the inner struggles that still exist for most of you.

You are all here by choice, and we are with you, supporting you and the transformation you are carrying out. Support one another so that the path will be easier. Open your hearts so that you can open the hearts of others and it will be easier for you to go through the changes. We bless you for coming here, and we here in Telos are celebrating because each of you is spreading the light to three, four, even six more people; in this way, we are fulfilling our Lemurian mission. The year 2012 opened a new gateway for humanity, a new opportunity for creation. Do you feel that there's no time? Indeed, there is no time; therefore, the awakening is happening rapidly. Dear ones, act today—don't put it off until tomorrow. Every decision must come from the heart and from the conditions in the present. Live the present at every given moment; now is the time to choose and decide; you are recognizing the vibration of choice and the decision is yours alone. The choice to ascend can change in a moment; therefore, you must make absolute choices at every given moment and preserve this energy.

Extraterrestrial Beings

Greetings, new-old friends. Welcome, this is Adama, High Priest of Telos, blessing you.

Yes, dear ones, at this time you are witnessing new energy entering the planet. The planet is filling with unique energy from a new place in the universe, far from the familiar central sun and planets. There is a universe that has awakened to the sounds of love coming from Planet Earth. Indeed, Planet Earth is at present disseminating its light throughout the cosmos. The new sounds are being heard far away, so that distant universes are awakening and listening to your heartfelt requests; your hearts are calling for light, for love, and for help in restoring the planet. You must understand that very distant solar systems are sending teams to restore the planet and increase the vibrations to such a level that a new energetic balance will be created that will make it possible for old friends to enter the atmosphere once again.

Dear ones, this is the time for you to open up to communication with these emissaries; this is the time for you to reconnect with ancient families. Yes, dear ones, it is the time. We are happy during these days when many friends are entering the planetary portals that have opened. A central planetary portal exists above Mt. Shasta; through this portal, extraterrestrials enter and leave the mountain. Some of you have been exposed to the activity above the mountain; some of you have even begun to create telepathic communication with these beings. You must let your heart instruct you and guide you to appropriate communication; you must feel the loving bond with these extraterrestrial beings. Indeed, their intentions are peaceful.

A new portal has recently opened above Egypt in the pyramids. This portal, which has been closed, has now opened again, and friends who have not visited the planet for a long time are beginning to return to the places they love, where they once had a connection with you, and harmoniously cooperated with you in the creation of a fifth dimensional life which you experienced in ancient eras.

Another portal is located above the light city Jerusalem. This portal is being prepared at present, but energetic cleansing is required before it is available for the entry of extraterrestrials into your region. The arrival of extraterrestrials will draw life in the frequency of the fifth dimension and higher, and thus support the process of planetary ascension. Part of your job, dear ones, is to help open these portals. The friends who enter via the portals are not taking over the planet; only those who have been here in the distant past and who know you, are invited. Their supervision is accomplished by the council whose intention is to rehabilitate the atmosphere, the oceans and seas, and the land; they intend to clean out the filth that has taken root, and help the earth's flora and fauna, which during the past decade, scarcely hold onto life, and return a state of growth and vitality to all living things.

Of course, among the friends there are those who enter your light bodies, and through you begin to change the reality and to fight against the powers of darkness. Indeed, this is the time of transformation. You must understand that we, from the light city Telos, are working in cooperation with those friends. Our goals are identical, and our knowledge is connected to that of these friends from distant universes. We are one; the plan is the plan of the Creator of worlds and universes, a plan intended to balance the entire system. This is why, dear ones, your awakening at this time is most important. Connect with your sacred heart; enter within. This is the time to ask the questions and open the codes; this is the time for working together as a group.

Telos Israel today is a broad base for sons of light to connect and work together for the sake of the planet, with love, generosity, and a sense of mission. Do you feel a sense of mission? Telos organizations worldwide are joining in an exciting union to strengthen the frequencies of the planet and turn them into frequencies of love and light; in this way, they are working toward the same desired change. Friends, now is the time to join the planetary mission; this is the year in which significant change will take place, and this is the time, dear ones, to awaken.

From Telos we appeal to each and every one of you. We call on you to connect with your energy vibration in the city of light, and in this way to strengthen the dormant places, open codes, and awaken to your role. Throughout the day, we send the violet ray to purify the planet, and the white ray for the ascension of humanity in these times. We send these rays to help you live in balance. Use them, dear ones, breathe in the flames, connect with your sacred heart.

Bless you, Adama

Meeting with the Pleiadians

Mt. Shasta, four o'clock in the morning. I wake up and connect to the guardians of the mountain, the little people who welcome me and tell me that tomorrow we will meet. They fill me with love and confidence, and I sit up and connect to the mountain. I see above it a gigantic space ship, enormous in size. I receive a blessing of peace, and it is explained to me that this space ship belongs to the Pleiadians, and that during the past two months they have been working with great energy in the mountain. This is why a gigantic cloud has been hovering over Mt. Shasta recently, causing haze and obstructing vision. I am invited to enter the spaceship and rise up in my etheric body. The commander of the ship welcomes me and suggests that I undergo an expansion of the brain and an opening of the DNA codes in my body, at a deep level. I thank him. I am led to a chair made of crystal combined with another material whose nature is unclear to me, and am seated. A dark violet ray penetrates my brain expanding it, and I feel my physical body stretching and have great difficulty breathing. The light continues to flow and combine with a golden color that fills all the particles of my body.

Adama arrives to make me feel secure; he explains the essence of the Pleiadians' role in these times, and tells me that there is cooperation between them. The charging continues and I feel protected. I see the commander. At the center of his chest lies a red crystal, emitting tremendous energy. I see how the crystal in my heart is also colored red, and receive the explanation that we can now communicate telepathically and work together. I return to myself and rise from the chair. They lower Adama and me through a beam of light deep, into the mountain. When we come to a stop, I see before us the Pleiadians' bases; gigantic dome-shaped structures, where they live in groups. I take leave of Adama and return to a state of full wakefulness. Tomorrow morning I will go to the mountain.

Conversation with the commander of the Pleiadian spaceship

Tell me who you are and what your role is in Mt. Shasta at this time.

First, we want to thank you for the connection with us, a connection that will bring about cooperation in raising the frequency of the planet. We Pleiadians are familiar to you human beings. We arrived from the Pleiades cluster of stars when the first groups of souls arrived on the earth, and we sowed our seeds so that we would be able to maintain life on this planet. Over time, there were changes in the plan of creation, but we won't go over that story. Today, we are present in a number of energetic portals, including Mt. Shasta. We are also present in the Middle East and above Tibet. Our goal is to continue the work with Mother Earth.

The flora and fauna on this planet are at an end stage of life, and we are examining which of the species we planted here have withstood the third dimension and which have not. We are learning the story of the planet, absorbing from trees thousands of years old, the frequencies that existed here, and learning from animals about evolutionary changes. We are gathering the memories of flora and fauna from different eras the planet has experienced and studying how, with the shift of the planet into the fifth dimension, we can reroot species that existed in the past and are worth restoring. We are also taking part in climate changes on the planet; there will be another adjustment of half a degree in the angle of the planet. These planetary changes will alter the regional climates—desert areas will become more fertile, the tropics will become sub-tropics, and so forth. The polar areas will also change. We are helping Mother Gaia, Mother Earth, to get through the final steps of parting from the old, and building the new. In this process, there will also be energetic purges manifested on the planet; some human beings will take leave of the planet.

This is indeed the way things are. Telos is reaching for a frequency higher than the fifth dimension, up to and beyond the eighth dimension. Some of the people from the city will connect with human beings who have succeeded in making the transition to the fifth dimension. These changes will take place in the coming fifty years, according to the timing of the planet. We are working today with many sons of light on the planet, and we are happy to see the change taking place in the human species. Many will pass to the level of consciousness of the fifth dimension, but we also see that many others will not. Unlike you, we live in groups; our consciousness is of the group; hence, there is a difference in our way of life. We are again establishing colonies on the planet, but we know this is temporary.

The consciousness of human beings has risen extensively of late; we are examining to what degree you act from your sacred heart in all ways, not just cognitively, as you did in the days of Atlantis. Without the heart energy, the planet cannot ascend; only when your hearts connect to one another will there be union and work through sharing, and only then will you be able to ascend as a race. Therefore, many of you are receiving messages; those who are unable to release the karma of control, of ego and of other negative human characteristics will leave the game. We are happy that a channel of communication has opened up between us; we are at the beginning of a shared journey.

Peace to you, old-new friend, Dominion, commander of the mother ship Shasta.

The Sixth Level

Dear ones, the sixth level in Telos is located at the base of the city, and we invite you to enter and accelerate the raising of the vibration. Of course, in order to enter the sixth level you will first have to undergo purification in the seven central flames, as we worked with them in Telos last year. The sixth dimension opens access to the codes that anchor energies at the highest spiritual level and return you to full balance and gentle purity. When you return from the sixth level, you will have to be focused in order not to be sucked back into the events of the third dimension. Remember that after your visit, you will need to drink water so that the purification you undergo will continue to the seventh level. The codes are given to all light workers who devote themselves to the mission and to the new way of life on the planet. The sixth level is open, and more and more codes will be transmitted.

When you enter the gateway of the sixth level and are in the quartz temple, sit on the crystal chairs and breathe deeply. The chairs give off high vibrations that will connect you to the energy and etheric bodies; in this way, channels will open for receiving future messages and codes. Every light entity is open to receiving the codes and renewed awakening. Your light bodies are conductors; the codes enter into the molecules of light, are collected within them and are stored in the light centers of your body—the chakras. These days the chakras are not only opening and being purified, they are also becoming the central carriers of the codes. Every area in the body receives encoding for opening the physical, mental, emotional, and etheric body, and through the opening chakras, your bodies become conductors that function in the fifth dimension.

Light groups that reach Mt. Shasta go through the steps intended to prepare the body to absorb the high vibrations in the mountain. Some of you have undergone encoding in other ways; however, the correct way, of course, is to visit the sixth level once a week, according to your own timing, and perform balancing work at that high level. We are happy that many of the sons of light in your area can reach the sixth dimension. The vibrations in your area are rising rapidly, and the changes occurring in the Middle East can be clearly seen. Vibration levels are rising and influencing the light, which is more plentiful than ever before.

We invite you to enter all the levels in the light city Telos. Keep up your work faithfully. Bless you, Adama, the High Priest from Telos.

Meditation:
a Visit to the Sixth Level

We breathe deeply. We get into a carriage that travels at the speed of light. The carriage turns west, and we pass over oceans and continents and connect with a beam of yellow light that comes from the center of the universe and connects to Mt. Shasta.

We descend deep into the mountain. The carriage stops, and when we get out, a guide from Telos welcomes us. We follow him along a path of beautiful colored bricks made of crystal.

The winding path takes us to yellow lifts built like capsules. We enter the lifts and go down, to the depth of the sixth level. Further and further down we go, and when the capsules stop, we get out. We all walk in a group behind the guide. An immense yellow, transparent pyramid stands before us. Its doors open wide, and we go up thirteen steps and enter it. At the center of the pyramid burns the golden flame. We stand around it, breathing deeply and feeling the flame permeate every cell and every atom and electron in our physical, mental, emotional, and etheric bodies. We feel the expansion.

Each of us is invited to sit on a crystal chair; from the base of the flame emerge crimson threads that make their way into our sacred heart. We feel them entering deep inside and creating circles of a new frequency the likes of which we have never felt. The heart chakra fills with the frequency of the flame and heals every doubt and every sensation that prevents us from being in balance. The flame dissolves every pain and heals those places in our hearts that still need healing. Particles of a new life are being created and shaped. The crimson thread continues down to the chakra of the solar plexus, purifying it in a circular manner and filling it with bright golden light, opening blockages and dissolving every compressed feeling that exists in the area.

Let's take a deep breath.

The crimson thread continues to the base chakra and enters the center of the kundalini; see how the kundalini is filled with golden light, and how the two snakes of the kundalini raise the frequency of the flame along the spine, filling up the area in a circular manner, with a bright golden light, opening, expanding, and ventilating the chakra.

Another crimson thread reaches the throat chakra and fills the area with the frequency of the flame. The flame creates anew the energetic center and introduces a frequency of creation, brightness, and lucidity. The chakra is shaped into an illuminated ball of golden light that expands and opens the area. Another thread goes out to the third eye, which the golden flame fills with soft, golden light. The light is somewhat dazzling, but causes the center to open to multi-dimensional vision, which is increasing at this time.

The crimson thread reaches the crown chakra. It cleans the petals of the lotus flower situated above the crown chakra, and all the petals of the flower open and fill with bright light, growing and expanding.

We breathe in deeply. The thread of the flame now enters all the DNA helices and rouses them; the codes awaken and open.

The golden flame has qualities of renewed creation. It is powerful and works quickly, streaming to our light bodies the powerful frequency of protons and electrons that are charged with electromagnetic energy; this accelerates and causes the movement of magnetism in our physical and etheric bodies. These actions bring about the creation of choice in our patterns of thought. Our light molecules awaken, open, expand, and thicken, and together they join to form a renewed creation.

Now we breathe in deeply and feel our bodies growing stronger and uniting into one. We see our energy centers immersed in a golden color, and a sense of empowerment fills our body. We take our leave of the flame and the temple, rise in the yellow capsules, enter the waiting carriage as a group, and continue to connect with the beam of yellow light rising out of Mt. Shasta.

The Golden Flame

The veil has been lifted; the veil that for thousands of years has separated the world of humans from the world of angels, masters and loved ones. The planet is experiencing a change, and humans are awakening, longing for a change in politics, economy, education, et al.

How can we take part in this change?

We can take part through our awareness, our thoughts, and speech and through appropriate communication with each other. We can take part by doing. We are not alone in this change—new-old flames are entering the planet, cleansing, accelerating, healing, and charging. When we see the magic, we wonder, we try, we focus, and we experience change in our creation manifesting in our lives.

Welcome. This is Adama, the priest from Telos, who welcomes you, dear ones, on the journey of enlightenment. In these sacred days, we invite you to expose yourself to the golden flame as it strikes the planet to cleanse your light bodies. The flame is ushering in the golden era. With the opening of the portals, the golden frequency is entering the planet. Many of you see it surrounding you and feel its potency. This flame accelerates time, cleanses your planet, and prepares you, dear ones, for the transition between dimensions.

The golden flame is one of the flames that have recently revealed themselves to humanity. You already know of the seven flames; this is the eighth one. The temple of this flame exists in the Middle East above the city of Jerusalem, heavenly Jerusalem, golden Jerusalem, the light city that is made of pure gold. This Jerusalem has golden gates that open to the tender sound of harps playing. Indeed, King David's harp in ancient times transmitted frequencies for opening the city gates. Today, dear ones, the city keys are in your sacred heart, in the pure heart that has the power to play the tones of peace to open the gates so that the children of light can enter the city of God. At the center of Jerusalem, stands the temple of the golden flame. Within is the golden flame, bright and shining in its beauty, with its powerful frequencies. Those few who can withstand the high frequency are invited to stand and breathe its light.

The essence of the golden flame can also be found in its temple in Telos, in the sixth dimension. The flame is descending to our planet at this time. The golden flame has the capacity to illuminate all our bodies. It penetrates all the light cells in our crystal bodies and accelerates their energy. When we enter this frequency, the flame brings in a great amount of creative energy, which accelerates tenfold the process of expanding our crystal bodies. The golden flame flows through our bodies—the physical, mental, emotional, and spiritual—healing and accelerating the electromagnetic flow, so they can take part in the co-creation of reality.

This is accomplished by using the soul star chakra, located above the crown chakra and connected to the higher self. The flame is reaching those children of light who have opened all their energy centers and are ready to absorb its powerful frequency.

At present, it is recommended to use the golden flame with another flame, in order to deepen the healing. The golden flame helps the body assimilate its healing qualities in order to renew itself and rebuild and regenerate body and nerve cells. It helps open the dormant cells in our brain so that we can use a higher percentage of them.

Many of you are connecting with this flame at present and see it burst forth in front of your very eyes. You feel its powerful frequency. The flame is cleansing the light cities and the chakras of the planet. I invite you to a journey of union in the temple of this flame in Telos.

You descend to the heart of Telos, which is washed in the light of the eternal flame. The flame is situated at the center of the city plaza, shining with beauty and strength, and radiating the crystal frequency of love. Breathe deeply and feel the frequency of the flame entering your tender crystal body, entering all its light particles. Breathe deeply; let your body expand as it fills with air. Feel the lightness.

You stand around the flame in a circle, joined by friends, family members from Telos, and children of Lemuria who carry the frequency of light in their being. They bear the heritage and culture of Lemuria, and through their contact with you, they support your being and accompany you on your journey of awakening into the light. As we stand here in a circle, the energy that surrounds your being connects us. The eternal flame continues sending its rays, enveloping you tenderly with love and joy. Breathe deeply into your sacred heart and enter with this frequency deep into the inner diamond in the depths of your soul. We are about to embark on an exciting journey to the sixth level, to the temple of the golden flame.

We all go down a path of crystal stones, accompanied by friends and guides, into the sixth level. The winding road leads to a lift made of crystal; we get inside it and descend deep into the earth, deep into the healing layer of the sixth level. Leaving the lift, we see before us a golden path leading to the golden temple. As we follow the meandering path, we already feel the growing frequency in our expanding light bodies.

We take a deep breath in order to contain the frequency that enters our body. Before us is the temple of the golden flame. It is huge and diamond shaped, made of transparent crystal, radiating golden sparks. We can feel the powerful frequency in our physical bodies. We climb the stairs and go to the center of the diamond. There, from the depths of the crystal, rises the golden flame. It ascends higher and higher; standing only a short distance away, we can feel its power. The flame, with its pure golden color, rises up to the vortex of the diamond. We are invited to sit around the flame in crystal chairs. When seated, we feel a golden flame coming down to our soul star chakra above the crown chakra. The ray is very fine and delicate. The flame enters the soul star grid in each one of us, building a connection with the cosmic creation, a connection with the creator. This chakra is made like the flower of life[5], but each one has an individual grid made of golden threads woven in this energetic center.

Breathe deeply and look closely; this is the light map of your being, and we each build our way according to the role our soul has chosen. The golden flame is powerful in its energetic charge, lighting up your personal grid and illuminating the connections that were not clear or were lacking in energy. Watch the grid being built and the connections being woven; see the grid carrying energy, life force, and power through it. This map continues to be formed with each experience that is assimilated into your body's cells; the grid continues to be built with each initiation, bearing your private frequency on your private journey, and carrying the codes of your soul. It is dynamic.

The ray continues on its way down to your crown chakra; the lotus flower opens up and is washed in a golden light that illuminates all the petals of the different levels of this energetic center. Each petal of the lotus represents the power of your soul to create in this life and manifest your creation. See the petals glow in golden light, see them thickening, and feel the creation nearing the realization of your vision, your destiny.

The light continues downward, cleansing the other chakras in its golden light, a pure light that enlivens each energetic center through which it passes. See how your

---

5 "the flower of life"- The flower of life is a geometrical shape composed of multiple evenly-spaced, overlapping circles arranged in a flower-like pattern with six-fold symmetry like a hexagon. The perfect form, proportion, and harmony has been known to philosophers, architects, and artist around the world. Pagans consider it to be sacred geometry containing ancient religious value depicting the fundamental forms of space and time

third eye opens to spiritual vision; see how the center of your thought chakra opens to appropriate expression of truth and integrity; see how the center of your heart opens to the frequency of love, compassion and acceptance; see your solar plexus open and release anger and behavior patterns that no longer serve you; unite with the sacral chakra, which connects with Mother Earth and stimulates creative ability and expression in your physical world. Take a deep breath. All the light particles in your etheric, emotional, mental, and spiritual bodies have awakened with the light of the golden flame, and as the light expands it strengthens them and clarifies the activities through this healing. In these moments you are surrounded by angels with golden crowns; as they stand before each one of you, love and light envelop you in this connection with your angel, and the angel gently transfers the golden crown to your head. This is the initiation crown of the golden flame.

We feel as if our body is floating in the power of this frequency. We give thanks from our sacred heart and depart from the golden flame temple. Our crystal body is immersed in golden light. With gratitude, we leave the sixth level, ascending in the crystal lifts to the center of Telos. Before us is an inter-dimensional portal. We say goodbye and pass through the portal. Filled with energetic power, we reunite with our physical bodies.

Breathe deeply and see all your bodies being reunited. Say three times, "I am that I am, I am that I am, I am that I am. Welcome back."

The Flame of Harmony

Welcome, this is Adama, the High Priest from Telos.

I bless you, sons of light, you who have walked together on the path of love, compassion, and ascension. We have accompanied you and continue to accompany you. Your sacred heart is opening like a rose, filling with the light and love of the universe that are flooding Planet Earth.

This is a time of celebration in all the worlds—celebration and love in many universes being built anew from the light that is increasing. Indeed, dear ones, a great light of life is emerging from the planet and uniting with the light of divinity, empowering the god particle in the central sun at the center of creation. Thus, the portal that has opened brings celebration and renewed creation for many worlds beyond your universe. Enlightenment is coming to your parallel lives and is touching your souls, which exist in different dimensions as different consciousnesses.

Friends from distant planets have arrived for this time of celebration. Many ships arrived in the light cities. Shamballa glowed with a powerful light and the inner diamond of Gaia was energized, flooding all levels of Gaia with light. Internal compressed energy was released; the rain and snow that fell in many parts of the planet were created to soften and refine the steam that emerged from the earth.

We have joined you in forming circles all across the planet, beginning with the entry of the sacred energy at midnight, and continuing until the opening of the portal at noon. The portal is still open and will remain open for two months. Human beings are continuing to awaken and feel the change that is taking place within them. The change is manifested in the physical body; some of you may feel your heart differently; you may feel fatigue while your physical body receives this powerful frequency. Community meetings are especially important at this time. This enables you to join other sons of light in performing light work on your body, on the levels of DNA that are awakening and continue to become more condensed, and in order for you to awaken the light codes in the chakra centers. Indeed, the more time you spend with fellow sons of light, the easier it will be for you to carry the new frequency.

How can we recognize the sons of light, you ask. Your sacred heart will direct and guide you to sons of light. Support one another at this time. Note where the frequency drops and enrich these surroundings with the frequency of love. It is possible that some of you will wander around your countries and even around the world. Indeed, many sons of light these days are returning to their origins; hence, many of you will feel the desire to move to a certain place, without even being aware of the inner need. The need comes from an ancient spiritual place; Gaia calls you so that you will be able to help and support the process of ascension in that place.

Beloved sons of light, the process is happening; the new world is being formed, and you will feel the changes in all the organizations and in all areas of your life. Humanity is returning to the days of the creation, to the days of Lemuria, where you functioned with ninety per cent of the DNA codes of your cosmic knowledge. As sons of Lemuria, as sons of the Maya, you are awakening at this time to an understanding available through the fifth dimension where the veil does not exist. Now allow yourselves to remove the limitations that still exist in your thoughts. Activate the pineal gland and the crystal brain, and allow yourselves to live connected with the divinity within you, connected with the One.

I invite you to an exciting meeting with Master Zohar.

I bless you, old friends. I observe everyone reading these lines of words; the energetic frequency enters your understanding and awakens your soul to the connection that has existed between us since ancient times, since the days of Lemuria, and even earlier. Indeed, I recognize you by the color of the frequency that comes from your aura. Are you aware of the importance of the aura that surrounds your body? Are you aware of the importance of what you eat and the importance of the quality of the water you drink? Are you aware of the damage you cause your aura by putting sugar, cigarette smoke, alcohol and drugs into your body? Are you aware of the negative effects of being close to people who drink alcohol, smoke, or who do not have an appropriate frequency?

I'll tell you a short story about a monk who was living in seclusion in a cave in Tibet. One day, the monk entered the cave and realized he was undergoing a test, a test of faith. The monk found a comfortable rock deep inside and sat feeling that this was a worthy place. He closed his eyes and entered a state of deep meditation; he connected to the beating of his heart, connected to his soul, connected to belief, connected to his angels, and little by little returned to breathe the breath of divinity coming from the prana entering the crown of his head. Thus, the monk sat for days on end without food or water, only breathing in the gentle breath of prana.

Thirty days passed, and an angel came to him and asked if he was interested in returning to a corporeal life. The monk answered that he was interested. "And what will you do in that life? Will you have need of your body?" asked the angel. "Yes," replied the monk, "for doing and creating, for achieving the joy of divinity from within my heart, for the love of the flora and fauna and for union with creation." Through his experience of being disconnected from his body, the monk realized the importance in this life of his choosing the living, breathing body, realizing that his body had many functions in the material world. He returned to breathing through his physical body, opening his eyes and returning to the third dimension. Together with the angel, he returned to the monastery and began to restore his body with food from Mother Earth, food that returned him to the physical body he had chosen, and he began to live a life of creativity and enjoyment.

And so it is with you, dear ones in the third dimension. Remember what you have chosen and what your role is at this time. You are not monks; you face many temptations. You are drawn to places that do not give you the ability to connect with your physical body and carry out your mission here on earth with integrity. Your body vibrates at a certain frequency. When you are not in balance, you cannot fulfill what you intended for yourselves. Indeed, this is a lesson of belief in your ability to create your way of life in your world. You no longer need to reach an extreme state in order to awaken or understand or accept; you must celebrate and enjoy life from your present state of consciousness. These days, I whisper to human beings anew; I come from the frequency of harmony; I come from the frequency of peace.

I arrived in the light city Telos some 12,000 years ago in order to support and help in the growth and development of the city. It is a beautiful and special city to all sons of light on the planet, especially to me. I invite you to a new temple that is revealed and open to humanity in the frequency of ascension and harmony; I invite you to enter the radiant healing temple.

Take three deep breaths and see how the white ray of light originating in the temple penetrates and floods the center of your crown chakra. The lotus opens and expands with the light of creation; see yourselves in the center of Telos, your etheric body illuminated and expanding. You are standing in the city center beside the eternal flame, a flame that transmits the frequency of infinite love at all times. Your heart expands and grows; your heart is open. Feel the serenity in your body.

We hover together, and your inner eyes already see the radiant temple. Observe its appearance; it is a pyramid of enormous size, made of crystals that radiate different shades of gold, silver, and brilliant white. See that the golden gate of the pyramid is open, and you are invited to pass through the arch in front of the pyramid. Take a deep breath and stand beneath it. The arch emits currents that enter your body, thoroughly purifying it; all that does not contain the frequency of love is discarded. Breathe deeply; allow everything that is needed to be drawn in, and what is not needed to be released.

You step forward and enter the radiant temple, and I am with you, loving and supporting you. Three priests stand before you, welcoming you, and bestowing upon you a blessing of peace. Each priest has a square chain of crystal made of gold, and as you enter, each of you receives a transparent crystal chain. This chain will help to moderate the powerful energies you will experience in the temple. Breathe deeply as you enter. Observe the many flowers blooming; observe the golden-silver waterfall that is flowing. Breathe deeply and enter the center of the pyramid. From deep within the crystal, emerges the flame of radiance, composed of three colors: brilliant white, the flame of ascension, the gold flame, and the silver flame.

This flame holds the flame of ascension, whose color is bright white and contains the seven sacred flames that create the quality of ascension into the fifth dimension, the powerful gold flame, a catalyst of energy entering the planet at this time, and the silver flame, which breaks up discordant energy and builds the energetic frequency appropriate for your body. The frequencies entering bodies must be compatible with one another, and sometimes they are too intense. The characteristics of the silver flame enable it to match its energy with the etheric body which exists in the fifth dimension, to activate the DNA in a way that is compatible with the crystal body, and to create unity among all the components creating the whole—your being.

Inhale the flame of radiance deeply; feel it permeating your entire being; breathe deeply and feel it penetrating all your cells, all your protons and electrons, your codes, your DNA and your heart. Breathe deeply; the light enters your energy centers and your heart. Great love floods you; you are loved and are blessed in this process. See the flame continuing to caress your being, and I, dear ones, pass from one to another, observing, supporting the process, and blessing.

Breathe deeply; the process is complete: your body has been charged in the flame of radiance, the flame of the firth dimension, the flame of the new world. You depart from the temple, the pyramid of radiance, descend the steps, return the crystal chains to the priests, and take your leave. A guide from the temple accompanies you to a path of crystal bricks, and back to the center of the light city Telos. You feel lightness, strength, purity, and wakefulness. You part company for now, cross through a multi-dimensional portal, and return to your physical body, to the here and now; you are full, exuberant, and joyful. Be on your way, dear ones.

Go out into the new world, the world of harmony in all areas of your life.

I bless you with the radiance of creation in your world.

Master Zohar[6]

---

6 Zohar is a very senior master from the city Shamballa inside Planet Earth. He has been on the planet, living in the same body, for some 250,000 years. He is about four-and-a-half meters tall, appears to be about 35 years old, and has bright white hair. He helped with the building of the Telos 12,000 years ago, when the Lemurians first moved there. Zohar says, "I have spent a lot of time in Telos over the past 12,000 years, especially at the beginning. I have learned to love this place just as I love my own city, Shamballa." (from *Protocols of the Fifth Dimension*, Aurelia Louise Jones, 2006).

The New Children

Welcome, this is Adama, the High Priest from Telos, greeting you.

In these times, these Messianic days, the world is full of new children—indigo children, crystal children, and rainbow children, bringing in the new vibrations of the energy to sustain Planet Earth.

Each of these children has a role and each one of them brings a special ray of light with which to help build a new society. These souls are making the highest divine choice in choosing to incarnate at this time. They consciously choose which ray of light to bring and which calling to follow. Indeed, the wonderful children of light are filling your society. We request your help, dear light workers. We are asking you to help these children to become integrated and to connect with their powers, so that they will be able to remember the knowledge they have gained and the choices they have made and will not be overwhelmed by the old energy. Accept them and include them. Help them dissolve the energetic knots and obstructions that appear in their chakras during adolescence.

Avoid giving them medications and unhealthy food, and bombarding them with electronic appliances. Give them the opportunity to connect with nature, creativity, music, and learning through experience. These children have an open pineal gland. They see everything through the third eye, hear voices differently from the way we do, and receive a wider range of transmissions. They feel things differently and their hearts are open and able to feel the hearts of others. These children have arrived with a clear purpose. We appeal to you to pave the way best suited for them and treat them with respect. Learn from them, speak to them heart to heart without judgment and ego. These children will break through the obstacles you are experiencing at this time; for them, everything is formed and ready, and their DNA is able to absorb twelve helices.

Two helices of DNA have been expanded to twelve through the light work we have done, and it will continue expanding to thirty-six. The children of today are already born with twelve DNA helices, and when the time is right, they will become active. In fact, they already exist in a somewhat dormant state, and the children must be helped, directed, and connected to their inner strengths. You are their teachers and they are your teachers.

Our children in Telos are different. Our light bodies have existed for hundreds of thousands of years, whereas at the present stage of development on the planet in the third dimension, life lasts only a short time. This period of childhood is very important, because the mind is very tender; it is vulnerable and absorbs any and all frequencies, including those that are not of love. When a child is nourished with love, the cells of the body develop maximally and attain self-fulfillment; when a child feeds on fear and anger and does not receive the love he needs, his development, mental and physical, is energetically blocked and stunted. Hence, caring properly for your children is of great importance.

In the city of Telos and in many other light cities, every being who wants to be a parent is examined in depth, and only with much guidance are light entities permitted to mate. The concept of "mating" is not the same as that in your dimension, but is rather mating in a spiritual sense, at the highest level of the soul. In any case, as has been mentioned in the Telos books, the decision to become a parent must come from the purest place and be undertaken with commitment to the process. The periods of pregnancy, birth, and rearing the light entity are also different from yours. In your world, the act of fertilization is performed many times and in haste, without intention and without the frequency of love, which must exist.

When a child is born in Telos, the entire city participates in the celebration. Many angels give protection and security to the newborn, and everyone also gives protection, love, and support. Teaching goes on throughout childhood. Thus, the children of Telos are not necessarily children, and among them are beings hundreds of years old. When the child reaches maturity, he enters the circle of giving to the community. Little by little, skills and professional capabilities are developed according to personal choice. In this way, the children of Telos are integrated into the society.

For some time now, the children of Telos have also been working with light entities from the third dimension, in order to provide a safety net of protection and support to beings who communicate with us in the fifth dimension. Similarly, the joint work of your children with the children of Telos is very important; when you bring your children to Telos, it is an opportunity for them to meet suitable groups of children who can support them, teach them, and connect them to the ancient knowledge that is already implanted in them.

Message from Matirion, a Mature Child from Telos

Peace to you, friends. I am Matirion, and although I am four hundred years old, I am still considered a child in Telos.

I am a mature child, a sort of guide in the childrens' society. I have already completed the forming of my emotional body, and I am equipped with love and confidence, compassion and generosity towards the community. I still have to complete acquiring the professional skills I will need when I become an adult light entity. Because of my skills and my tremendous desire to work with children in love, I have chosen to work in educating the children of Telos. At present, I am receiving training from the master, my teacher, who meets with me every day and instructs me. I am also part of a team of twelve children from Telos who are undergoing the same training I am, and we provide, as volunteers, support to light entities from the third dimension who wish to learn how to care for the light and disseminate it across humanity. We see great importance in this work, because in this way we connect with the goal of the Lemurian light entities in Telos in raising humanity's vibration.

Our spiritual-cosmic knowledge is also expanding, and we are studying in depth the cosmic lessons that are taking place at present on the planet. It is important to us to continue planting the knowledge in the younger children of Telos, some of whom will emerge in the future into the fifth dimension on the surface. Many children are undergoing special training for this purpose, as am I, but not all children of Telos are designated to emerge above ground.

Couplehood is an experience familiar to the children of Telos from a very early age. Until age thirty or forty, we experience couplehood that is not permanent; after that age, we enter long-term relationships. Our couplehood differs from yours because we have no commitment to stay with one light entity for an entire lifetime as you do. Of course, the length of your lives is very different from ours, hence your choice is different.

We bless you for your choosing change, and for the serious work you are doing. We are with you all the way, ready and happy to give you guidance in all matters related to the growth and care of children, and to working with them as well.

Transmitting Information: the Children of Light

Greetings, dear ones.

You must understand that your choice to come into the present incarnation was made after deep thought, and your light entity, which exists at the highest spiritual level, consciously chose to become embodied at this time, as have many others. The decision was the result not only of the aspiration for personal growth, but also out of the desire to help in the development of the planet.

A large number of the children arriving today are the light children who will lead humanity to correct the injustices that have occurred in recent centuries. Therefore, every soul who comes to earth at this time, out of a conscious choice to enter the limitations of the human body, is an extremely brave light soul. You must understand that in the stages of the journey that your souls are undergoing, there is a big difference between the third dimension and the fifth, sixth, seventh, and higher dimensions. Therefore, we, all the angels and masters, support the light entity and strengthen it in its first years, when its spiritual vision is completely open and it can see what is beyond the veil.

Today, as long as human society in the third dimension allows them to do so, the light children are empowering themselves and expanding the range of their inner vision and of their openness. Working with the light children is extremely important, and we appeal to all caregivers with a connection to light children, to allow the children to remain in the high spiritual awareness they are in at present, and to help them continue to seek vision and a connection "beyond the veil." Your educational institutions will also become more and more open to this subject in coming years. Of course, you are the leaders and the ground breakers; dare to change the old and turn it into new energy. We appeal to you, brave light souls who experienced a life of light in the days of ancient Lemuria, who have experienced love, harmony and a life of achievement. We ask that you continue to visit us in Telos, that you enter the temples of the flames and perform daily light work that will empower you until you realize your personal mission.

Personal development is of course important, but no less important is the collective purpose in which you have an important role. You must each therefore do your job and help raise the vibration on the surface and across humanity. Make use of the unique meditations presented to you, sit at least ten minutes a day, and connect with your soul. We will join you and support you at every stage of development. Connect with your heart, and think from within your heart.

With love, children of Telos.

Education

Greetings, dear ones, this is Adama.

The schools in which you "deposit" your children for most of the day need refreshing, renewal and change—change that involves awakening and awareness in all areas, from the administration, teachers and students, curriculum content as well as the physical setting. The educational system is one of the most important organizations in Telos, since every boy and girl go through a course of training, study, understanding and development that includes knowledge of the different bodies that make up the being who comes into this incarnation. When these beings choose to arrive, they receive two teams of parents—the energetic parents who create the being through an energetic connection of love, and the parents who accompany them in their early life, which can number in the hundreds of years. You must understand, dear ones, that the responsibility is shared, and the entire community supports the children in a variety of ways.

The first stage of nurturing is one of choice and of reaching out for the fifth dimension. Children arrive from a place higher than the fifth dimension, so they too undergo phases of adaptation. In the first years of their existence, they are exposed only to especially delicate vibrations; they live in places that contain color, music, and love, until their skin cells are filled with the vibration of the fifth dimension. Following this, the children are transferred to the development center for their first meeting with others their age. This center is like your kindergartens, except that we surround every three light souls with three adult escorts, so that each entity receives full attention. This is important because this period requires constant supervision to assure that the energy in which the child arrives will remain clear and pure. Thus, the first years of learning involve experiencing many different things.

In the next years, the children join others their age, while receiving constant support from their parents. Through experience and learning, they acquire the cosmic knowledge appropriate to the development of their path and personal mission. Indeed, even at this early age, the mission of each entity who willingly descends to the Telos community is determined.

The classrooms of the different age groups are constructed as inviting spaces for the children to be in. The rooms carry a frequency of love, knowledge, and curiosity, and each child is supported at all times by a personal instructor who reinforces the learning process. As noted, each child has a personal path, and each learns with appropriate masters. Throughout this period, the young beings connect with nature and animals, each one bonding with a particular animal that serves as an additional guide.

Next in the initiation of children of Telos as light entities in the fifth dimension and above, is the "fitness course," which teaches the importance of acquiring knowledge, and during which each entity acquires personal experience. When the children are learning about the universe and expansion of the stars, they travel through the expanse of time and across portals and dimensions, always escorted by their guides and teachers. The bond between guide and child is a soul connection. While acquiring knowledge, the children also engage in group activities with others of the same age. In their shared journey, the group must accomplish joint tasks. Cooperation between the children in the group is vitally important. Through working together, the children learn to practice compassion, giving, sharing, acceptance, and more.

We in Telos integrate children from both poles of the feminine and the masculine energies. There is no separation, so each entity learns to find the absolute balance between feminine and masculine aspects in adult life. During adolescence, we allow the children more and more freedom, and the guide gradually disengages from the child he has been accompanying. Freedom is essential at this age because the children themselves choose the lessons they will undertake on their personal path. We adults must direct, support, and teach the children.

There is a council for each age-level, which supervises the children of that age and follows their progress along their personal path. At the age of thirty, the children begin to experiment with exchanging energies of sex. We allow complete freedom in this exchange, and teach them how to balance the feminine and masculine energetic sides, preserving the whole. This period lasts about thirty years.

The children reach maturity after a long apprenticeship lasting throughout their adolescent years. During this period, they become more professional individually, each choosing an occupation for adult life, and how they will contribute to the community. Our community life is based on contributing and giving; each being gives about three hours a day to the community, and works in their profession about five hours. After this, each being devotes his or her time, every day, to development in the soul-spirit dimension.

Dear ones, the third dimension is taking on the laws of the universe, the laws of ascension, and the laws of the firth dimension. We are witnessing light groups performing energetic work to soften the energies of rigid organizations that still exist, such as the Department of Education. These organizations are absorbing the incoming energies. The change will indeed begin to appear, and it will happen among the children. Of course, change takes place throughout society. Your society is being rebuilt with attention to changing the way individuals are educated, as a community, as a national entity, and as a planetary entity. In the next thirty years, great change will take place. Now is the time to take responsibility, to reach out to circles of light and take action, dear ones, to change the reality that has been created on the planet, the only planet of choice. This is the time to choose anew the manner in which your children will be educated, the way in which you bring them up, and your way of life. The planet is being flooded with energies of the fifth dimension and the violet flame. Connect with these energies, and spread your light.

With you hand in hand, Adama.

A Trip Around Telos: Meeting the Children

At one of my Astral Journeys, I entered the level where the children of Telos can be found. Before me, I saw an expanse of grass, flowers, and trees. I walked along a winding path made of crystal bricks, which brought me to a gentle slope down to a beautiful, lightly flowing stream. From a distance, I saw an enormous oak tree, and around it the children were sitting in a circle; they appeared to be aged ten to thirteen. I approached and greeted them. In front of the children stood an instructor who was explaining how they could build energy devices by charging crystals exposed to sunlight for a long time, and then connecting them to the center of Mother Earth. Observing the children of Telos, I saw that they were listening and concentrating, and they were clearly learning through acceptance, comprehension, and sharing.

After the instructor had completed his explanation, the children formed creative work-groups in which they simulated charging the crystal. The instructor supervised them in the process, which involved connecting with Mother

Earth. The children went out into the open spaces to look for the right crystal for the group, and when they had a question, they posed it to the instructor telepathically.

I asked the instructor how it was that they worked together so well and that they were so quiet and attentive. The instructor answered that I was meeting them in the middle of the day, after they had already engaged, since first thing in the morning, in inner reflection and healing exercises in the healing pool or in the healing temples of the flames. He explained that the entire morning is devoted to balancing the children. At this age their frequency is very high, as energies enter their bodies at a fast rate; however, with the healing and the inner reflection, they are balanced when they arrive for their lessons. He added that they devote some five hours to these activities every morning, supervised and supported by the guide who accompanies the children from the moment they are born.

I thanked the instructor and continued on to another group. I entered a classroom in the shape of a half-dome made of hexagonal crystals. The children in the group, aged eighteen to twenty, sat on chairs made of crystal. In the center of the circle were a large table and a crystal ball. The instructor also stood in the center of the circle. I looked on and listened from the side. The discussion was about the role of the soul that has chosen to actualize itself as an entity in the light city Telos. They also discussed the connection to an additional part of the soul that has entered a physical body, and how worthwhile it is in these times to connect with the physical form. Everyone present was asked to visualize their parallel physical form and to feel the state of his or her consciousness and frequency.

It was explained to me that in these times, many sons of light in all the light cities are emerging with their being and connecting with their physical form. In this way, they raise the body's energetic frequency and create rapid awakening which leads to important action for the planet. This is a group selected to devote themselves to supporting humanity and helping with the ascension of the human sons of light.

The frequency in the room was high, enveloping, and loving, and I felt their strong intention and desire to support humans at this time. My heart swelled with joy. I thanked the group and went out into the open spaces of Telos. My heart took me to another domed circle, a circle painted pink. From within the domed circle, a spiral of pink rays was emerging. As I approached, I felt my heart chakra expanding. I entered the circle; before me appeared young toddlers accompanied by personal caregivers. They were only a few months old, and they were already walking on their own two feet! Their bodies were larger than those of our children, and their sparkling chakras were clearly visible and open and possessed energy of a very delicate frequency. When I entered, a caregiver came and passed her hands over all of my body in order to check the frequency and further open my heart chakra. She performed a cleansing on my body, and I felt as if it were becoming soft and gentle. When I entered, the children came up to me and welcomed me telepathically. There was a frequency of affection in the room.

The various crystals in the room were round and soft, full of a liquid substance; the children moved among them, approached them, hugged them, spoke with them, and released their feelings. The room filled with laughter, light, and much love. It was explained to me that the children spent most of the day out in nature, and now were undergoing a process of connecting with the crystal frequency in their bodies, a very delicate frequency that helped them connect with this vibration. It was also explained that they each received close individual supervision throughout the day, and that their nutrition was light and included very delicate foods, at this stage, because their bodies were delicate. Until age three, most of their nourishment is energetic food composed of the parent's heart frequency and transmitted to the child's heart in the babies' growth and development temples. When they reach age three, they begin to eat more dense food.

I thanked the leader of the group and the babies, and sent a ray of love to the gentle heart of each of them. I felt the ray softly returning to me from each of the little ones. I understood that their soul is connected to their being, that they are connected to high spiritual places, and that, despite their young bodies, their wisdom is great.

I left and went to visit my friend Duniyao in a village outside the city. I met Duniyao on my first journey to Telos, when I was invited to visit this village. She met me at the entrance and invited me to her home, a round house made of crystal in which there were a few rooms, a living room and a kitchen. In the village, most of the houses are transparent from the inside out; each family has a personal shrine beside the house, which is used for healing. Many times, I have sat with my friend in her kitchen, drinking pure crystal water and talking. During the two years I was in Telos as an emissary and volunteer, she accompanied and advised me. I thank her a thousand times for supporting and caring for me.

This time I met Duniyao beside a gigantic mulberry tree near the village. I approached her and we immediately exchanged greetings telepathically. Pink rays of light travelled from her heart to mine and back again from my heart to hers. My body expanded from the frequency of great love it received, and I felt as though my crystalline body was made of little diamonds vibrating at a powerful frequency that was expanding my consciousness.

Duniyao sat on the ground, and I did the same. She held in her hand a large transparent hexagonal crystal, and passing it to me, told me to hold it in both hands and look deep into it. As I observed it, I saw Ayelet in each of its facets in a different dimension. I saw Ayelet in the third dimension, but her frequency was lower than my frequency at present, and she was not in balance. Duniyao told me to look at the figure and speak to her higher soul. I started conversing with her being, and saw how the frequency was descending into Ayelet's brain and the brain was awakening. I sent her a shining ray of flame and saw the ray reach her sacred heart where it ignited a deep spark. I continued looking and saw another Ayelet, in the sixth dimension, a big Ayelet, enormous in her energetic dimensions, a figure filled with the frequency of love, compassion, sharing, harmony, and fulfillment. I asked her to connect with me and continue supporting me on my journey to ascension.

I asked Duniyao about the connection of all the parallel dimensions—are they in touch with one another? Duniyao answered that our light bodies and our physical bodies, which are at a dense level of consciousness, are more or less connected to one another at the highest level of the soul, and that there sometimes exists between them a shared state of consciousness. She added that sometimes one of our aspects is released from the physical body more quickly than the others, and it connects with energy to the place in need of energetic support.

Harmony and recognition among all the parts of our "I AM" presence in the parallel dimensions is possible at this time, and is important because when all the dimensions merge, it is possible to attain ascension beyond the physical body. Duniyao went on to explain that now is the time to become friendly with our self in the parallel dimensions, and join it to our self in the present dimension. "Not everyone has beings in the higher dimensions," she said, "but when one of your beings awakens, it helps the awakening and the growth of all your aspects in the different dimensions. When you have a being in a parallel world whose frequency is lower, its frequency will rise."

I thanked Duniyao, and saw before me my own figure from Telos approaching me. My heart began to expand; I felt my consciousness growing and my body expanding. My figure arrived and stood before me and we merged into one.

The Role of Women

We are glad of the opportunity to transmit to you, human beings, knowledge that is important and vital to continued growth and to raising the vibrations on Planet Earth. Mother Earth has already begun the journey of transformation and has raised her vibrations. Many light entities have begun an essential change with the goal of preparing their bodies for the fifth dimension, which is the dimension of light and love, compassion and giving. In the fifth dimension, positive thoughts are formed because thinking is aligned with the frequency of love and with the creation of pure energy through the heart chakra. In these times, strong feminine energy is resonating with heart vibrations because many women in the third dimension are seeking the light. Many men are also going through significant changes, and are opening up to these frequencies. For many long years, the feminine vibration on Planet Earth has been suppressed. At present, many souls are recalling an age in which there was no suppression and they were free of domination. These souls are now attracted to this powerful energy and are again connecting to freedom and the ability to choose.

Although there is male energy in women, their physical build is different from that of men. The make-up of their protons, electrons, and hormones is different as well. Women have always been connected to intuition and to the heart, even though for many incarnations they placed an inner and an outer block to these sacred abilities. The connection of women to Mother Earth is immediate; they identify with the energy of Mother Earth because they themselves are mothers, and in bringing the fruit of their womb into the world, they experience the feeling of unconditional giving. Because of this natural ability to embrace compassion and love, to give of themselves and devote themselves to others, many women in ancient times served as priestesses, healers, and caregivers.

Because of these feminine qualities, it is women who lead the movement toward the light. In recent centuries, women have fought to achieve freedom, and to this end have sacrificed their femininity. They have repressed their feminine characteristics in order to draw nearer to male energy. Now it is time to reconnect to the feminine energies. Say "yes" to gentleness and giving and "no" to warfare, ego, and domination. The feminine side is essential to the changes taking place today on Planet Earth.

In ancient times, women perceived life through their sacred hearts, and through their feminine relationships helped to preserve balance on the planet with a warm heart. Today, now that women have regained their understanding of the great importance of pursuing and spreading the path of light, they will no doubt influence their near and more distant surroundings.

To our regret, partnerships between men and women are not yet practiced properly on the planet. A man living alongside a woman is exposed to the feminine side and to light work and so he changes. In fact, many men today are already undergoing change in childhood, because male babies born these days are born into the new vibration and are more open and prepared to absorb the new energy on Planet Earth. These babies will grow into children who can reach the fifth dimension and will certainly get through 2012 easily. Older men, on the other hand, those born before the changes began and those who do not have a spiritual practice, are liable to experience great difficulty.

We call upon you women to continue leading society, family, and comrade-brothers, and to send out the violet light ray of love so that the change taking place around you can reach more and more people. We call upon you to unite and form light groups. It is important that men too participate in these light groups to balance the energy.

Women in the Middle East have been oppressed for thousands of years, and in most of the neighboring states in the region, women today are still oppressed and deprived of their rights. We call upon these women to unite and jointly perform personal and group light work in order to realign the energies to reduce the hold of male domination. An important lesson will happen in Iran, where the women will bring about a revolution that will begin small but will spread to the entire region.

We bless you dear women, brave goddesses. Continue to spread your light, which comes from an ancient time, the time of creation.

With love to your sacred hearts,
Adama and the Priestesses of Creation

Message from Lady Nada [7]

Good evening, women, this is Nada.

I have come here to talk with you about your feminine energy and the physical and energetic changes you are undergoing these days. The feminine aspect is changing, and you must be aware of this so that you can continue to work with us with your feminine energy and masculine energy in balance. Feminine energy is round, creative energy, and it holds within it motherly love, which you express in many ways in your lives. Energy in this form is attuned to the lunar cycle; it is no accident that the moon appears and disappears, and it is no accident that you have a monthly cycle. Connect with the lunar cycle as your mothers did in ancient times; pay attention to the dates and the cyclicality, and purify yourselves in a water source at the end of your period. This has a purpose. Do not treat your body like a machine; feel what it experiences; be sure it is in balance, clean and pure. In this way, you will be able to contain the

---

[7] Lady Nada served for a long period with Sananda (Jesus) working on the sixth ray, and has walked with him in the path of peace and love through many incarnations.

new vibrations entering Mother Earth, and be in harmony with the development of the soul and the growth of the "I AM" presence.

A clean, pure body can more easily contain the pure soul and be open to the new vibrations; it can absorb the frequencies of the fifth dimension, the insights, and the connection to the divine source. Pay attention to the food you eat. The nourishment you need is different from that of men. Women need to eat various plants and spices that help balance their energies. Go to the writings of Maimonides, Nahmanides, and other sources for help in creating balance.

Connect with the masculine energy that was once associated with hunting and is today associated with action and acquiring the material goods needed for your everyday existence. In order to connect with the masculine side, observe men, their eating habits, and their behavior. Even if their responses do not always find your approval, note that they are focused and do not tend to fall into drama. This energy can balance you.

Meditation: Temple of the Priestesses

Take a deep breath. We seat ourselves in a carriage, and it rises higher and higher and connects with a beam of yellow light descending from a source in the center of the universe. We rise with the carriage, and when we reach the light city Telos, the carriage opens and a guide from Telos named Julianne greets us, "Welcome dear ones, daughters of light, you are invited to follow me." We walk as a group behind the tall, enchanting guide, whose etheric body towers to a height of several meters, and her hair waves with every movement of her body. Her body is delicate, and when she hovers, we hover behind her and savor the aroma of jasmine surrounding us.

We continue until we reach a beautiful crystal building in the form of a heart and enter the rounded building. This building contains a soft, loving frequency, the frequency of femininity; pink, violet, lilac, turquoise, sunset orange, and other beautiful hues flood the place, and music is playing. We follow the guide deep inside, and when we reach the center of the temple, we sit down in a circle.

A golden ray of light penetrates each of us through the crown chakra, filling each and every cell of our bodies. The body expands and opens to the frequency of creation; DNA helices accelerate their resonance. We continue to breathe deeply and feel how the center of our sacred heart is expanding and growing. Each of us sends a pink ray from the center of her hearts, and in the center of the circle we build one heart that concentrates all the frequencies of the group. We are one. The heart in the center emits the frequency of the flame of love, and we feel our heart expanding and growing; we feel compassion, openness, and giving, and we feel that we are mothers and sisters and that we are caring and loving. Perhaps a sense of victimhood or control will also arise, but we are dissolving any energy that does not serve us. Any low frequency within us is washed away by the frequency of love, which cleans, connects, and creates the frequency of femininity—a clean frequency of unconditional universal love.

At present we are joined by priestesses from the temple, the masters Mary Magdalene, Lady Nada, Quan Yin the beautiful, and also the shaman Shaouti the wise. We stand beside them. In the center of the circle, we see the planet, blue and beautiful; we hold out our hands to it and fill it with frequencies of compassion, love and peace, healing and acceptance, and the frequency of creation. The planet fills with the pink rays of light coming from our hands, and it is now illuminated, warm, and full of the frequency of femininity, the frequency of unity and harmony.

We feel a special figure standing behind us and our hearts expand with excitement. When we turn around, we see before us our form from ancient Lemuria, the goddess and the priestess we chose to become in those days. We feel the connection and see our being merging gently with the figure. We breathe our unified breath, our one breath, merging with every cell and every atom and electron and joining our hearts, connecting with our memories and turning our vision into one. The figure connects with us and we leave the center of the temple, thanking all the divas, priestesses, and masters who have accompanied us in this process, and enter the carriage once again. We are serene; we are one with the figure of the goddess and with our being. This connection will last as long as we wish it to, and the answers are within us; we are invited to ask our divine being any questions we like. The carriage closes and rises again toward the exit from the city of light. It connects to the beam of yellow light and we are inside, rising higher and higher, and returning to this life enlightened, returning with inner strength and a connection to the goddess.

The Energy of Sex

Greetings, dear ones, this is Adama.

The energy of sex had a certain essence in the past, but it has been distorted over the years by human beings; it is power and control that have distorted the essence of this energy.

In ancient times, at the time of the creation, the time of Lemuria, each light body was charged with both energies, male and female. The combination of these two energies is essential to managing the light body, since in each there are different particles of creation, male and female, which originated with the Creator. Male particles are charged with ions, the essence of which are creation, action and control, whereas in female particles, the energy is of compassion, love, giving and openness. Only when there is a balance between these energies is it possible to achieve the intended ascension. In the past, a balance existed because creation was present in all light entities, and when one light entity chose to join with another for a shared charging of energy, the union happened in all levels of protons and electrons in the light bodies. The connection between the light bodies sometimes caused a tremendous explosion, and the spark that was created could be seen from afar. Through this connection, the beings were charged with light energy.

In your world, a short circuit has occurred through the energetic overload that is created when one system exerts dominating power over another. For tens of thousands of years, while the veil was lowered and the link to the creation was broken, your energetic reserves were depleted and your bodies were almost completely disconnected from the energy of creation. A limited source of energy remained which enabled functioning in the third dimension; thus, the exchange between male and female energies as it had existed was ended, and all that is left is the low energy connection in your etheric body at the base chakra. The entire area remains dormant. The energies no longer pass through the kundalini, and in effect, the sexual connection that you know today remains devoid of energy. It is used only for the propagation of the human species. During these dormant years, male energy has overpowered the female, so that for tens of thousands of years, women have been controlled by men in everything related to sex.

Today the human species is attempting to balance the female and male energies; often the male energy in a human body is more dominant, attracting to itself the opposite energy, the female, which it lacks. Thus we find the form of partnership common on your planet—a human with male energy, a man, together with a human with female energy, a woman.

You have seen in recent years that changes are taking place on the planet. We find couplehood between people of the same sex—a man with a man, a woman with a woman. This energetic connection is created when the dominant energy attracts to it the energy it lacks for balance. For example, if the dominant energy in the body of a woman is male energy, the woman may be attracted to female energy; or if the dominant energy in a man's body is female, he may be attracted to male energy. From your point of view, they form a same-sex relationship, but in fact, they are seeking balance. You must understand that a body that is out of balance, before it is attracted to a partner, must bring itself to a state of inner balance between the two energies, the female and the male. Indeed, that is how things are in our world; we maintain energetic partnership with a certain sex only after we have examined the energetic balance within our own light body and know to which energy we are attracted. Sometimes the attraction is to a light being with dominant male energy, and sometimes it is to a light being with dominant female energy.

In Telos, we grant young light beings the possibility of experimenting with partnership through the energy of sex when they reach their twenties or thirties. The subject of sex is taught in stages, because at certain times the energetic connection can create a powerful explosion. Anyone exposed to this energy must have suitable experience if they are to go through it in the correct manner; hence, they begin acquiring this experience at an early age. The learning process begins at age twelve and culminates between the ages of twenty or thirty, when they reach a harmonious union of sexual energies. This corresponds to the physical transition you experience from childhood to adulthood.

The apprenticeship and study leading to a final connection of all the light centers and the creation of energetic union takes place in several stages:

First, becoming acquainted with the two energies that exist in the being is the beginning step. At this time, we acknowledge the male energy that exists within us, associated with the blue flame, and the female energy that exists within us, associated with the pink flame. Each of the flames penetrates our sacred heart flooding all the energy centers, and through them, we learn to connect with the vibrations of creation. Through the male blue energy we learn control, focusing on goals and action; through the female pink energy, we learn compassion, giving, gentleness, love, and acceptance. The combination and the balance between the two energies lead to transmutation and create the violet flame, enlightenment, and ascension.

In the second stage, youngsters play with the energies, thereby testing when they are acting from a state of balance and when they are not. An adult in Telos must always be aware of the balance between the energies. A lack of balance disturbs harmony. On occasion, unpleasant events have occurred due to lack of balance, as in the case of Atlantis which became dominated by male energy. We aim to create completely harmonious states of being. Learning to maintain these states requires much time, so this second stage, in which the youngsters learn skills of energetic balancing, takes place over an extended period.

The third phase begins when young people begin to connect to beings with whom they can reach a state of balance. This is their first experience with the opposite energy that exists in a being outside themselves. Of course, the connection is supervised by an adult who guides the meetings and refines the energy so it is aligned for both beings. To this end, we have temples in the light city Telos for teaching this energetic balance. The youngsters usually begin acquiring skills through energy games, and gradually, over the years, become more aware and more skilled at identifying energies within the beings they encounter; they can tell by the vibration whether or not the being before them is in balance, and whether male or female.

The fourth stage is that of conscious choice, which comes after the games of acquaintance. At this point, adult beings at least twenty years of age choose one best in balance with themselves and with whom they want to realize a union. The meeting between the adult beings takes place in the hall of union, after they have done a thorough energetic balancing. They get to know one another, seeking the being with whom they can unite energetically. The first meetings arouse a good deal of excitement and these encounters are still supervised throughout by their instructors. When they reach the center of the temple, they are already in balance and begin to connect to the frequency of creation within themselves. The vibrations gradually rise, and with the connection to the center of the heart chakra, the chakra of creation, a great explosion of light takes place. The frequency of the energy is extremely powerful, and the beings expand to immense dimensions. The crystal hall is designed to contain the high frequencies.

Sometimes entities reach the temple of union in an unbalanced and unprepared state, and when the frequency rises and the connection to the centers of energy takes place, they are burned and injured. A being who has been burned is sometimes unable to function until their centers of energy and the personal frequency are rehabilitated.

The Energetic Connection— the Explosion of Love

The energetic connection of the light bodies creates a deep soul connection, which causes a tremendous burst of protons and electrons; these very quickly become currents of light carried beyond this and parallel universes.

The energetic meeting and connection between two light bodies takes place in the temple of union, which is a temple of love. The temple is pyramid-shaped; at its center, there is an energetic circle that the two beings enter (remember we are talking about light beings, not the physical form familiar to you). To begin, the energies merge and learn to exchange different frequencies between one another. Each of them balances the female and the male energies within their own being; when the balancing process ends, the beings begin to link the chakras, beginning with the base chakra. The kundalini awakens and a point of light is ignited within it. From there the energy rises to the solar chakra, which also awakens. The sacred heart chakra grows and expands, and circles of energy begin to open this chakra in each being. This center connects them to the love of creation. The energy continues to the throat chakra, and as the throat opens, some may make gentle sounds that support the process. The energy rises to the third eye chakra, a chakra that experiences colors yet to be seen in your world. From there, the energy rises to the shining crown chakra, enabling the energy of creation to flow to the beings. The energy continues to the chakra of divinity in a connection to the higher self and to the creator. The merging of the two is done in complete union.

This charging envelops the two beings and leads them into harmonious ascension. You must understand, dear ones, that this energy is sacred, and that this is the way in which new souls are created in our world; many beings in Telos were thus created, and they are sacred by virtue of the way in which they came into being. When two beings unite, the higher creation is present in their bond; this is a sacred occasion. Words cannot describe the power of this energetic meeting. The union is at the highest level of consciousness. The two beings become one, and from this moment, the connection between them is sacred. The encounter creates a great burst of light and a tremendous sound that can be seen and heard from afar. The light and the love frequency can be seen throughout Telos reaching all the energy centers in the city, and signaling that another sanctification has taken place.

A human body could not withstand the force of the high frequencies carried at the time of this encounter and connection; hence, the descent into physical bodies lowered the quality of sexual energies. The sexual connection experienced by physical human beings today is a far cry from the true connection created by God.

I accompany you on your way and bless you, Adama.

Balancing Sex Energy: Lesson 1

The High Priest Adama has entered the room, and he is about to deliver a message to us.

Welcome, you are blessed. This is Adama, High Priest from Telos.

I see the work you are doing and the hearts that are opening. You must understand, dear ones, that working with sexual energy is a gift. At this time, as you are becoming reacquainted with your bodies and all their energies, you are reawakening to the era of ancient Lemuria when physical bodies had the ability to contain great and powerful energy.

Sexual energy is one of the most powerful energies in the universe. You must understand that when you perform energetic balancing, you are charging your body so that you can fulfill your dreams, and pursue the things that interest you about the planet in a balanced state. You must also understand the sexual energy you are learning about at this time will be charged with the frequency of creation. The protons and electrons that will enter and accelerate the electromagnetic current in your bodies will allow you to expand and embrace more and more light. This is electrifying energy that strengthens you. Therefore, dear ones, you must take care to carry out the work you are doing with energetic balancing on a daily basis to maintain a balanced state.

Similarly, when you are working with sexual energy, you must be mentally mature. Your emotional state must also be in balance because sexual energy accelerates everything. Thus, when you are out of balance, the explosion of energy that comes with sexual interaction will cause you to become even more unbalanced. Therefore, dear ones, when you are opening your chakras, know that some of you, who still need to work on energy centers that are blocked, will be unable to contain this energy completely. Your work with sexual energy, therefore, is the initial work you are doing at this moment to process and balance your bodies, your energy centers, and your crystal bodies. This is energy that is assimilated and opens codes with every energetic process you undergo, such as opening the base chakra. You must understand that all those DNA helices have registered the energy that you have experienced in your physical, etheric, emotional, spiritual, and mental bodies. Even if you don't always understand it, know that the work is being done.

When you persevere with the process and continue working with energetic balancing of the female and male aspect in your bodies, you will be able to progress to the next step. Light work is daily work and the more strictly you perform it, the more your bodies will expand and contain a more powerful frequency of light. This is the path to the golden age; these are the steps in this process. In these times, you have the ability to learn these teachings and embrace your bodies. There were times when your physical bodies could not handle being exposed to a powerful frequency like that which is entering the planet at present; the bodies were sick, and weak, and injured. Sometimes you may feel fatigued with various aches and pains or a headache. Perform deep healing on yourselves through reiki, proper nourishment, drinking plenty of water, etc., so that you will be able to continue functioning and absorbing this great light.

Indeed, your family has guided you in the present meeting. From this place you are learning, receiving, and acquiring extensive hidden ancient knowledge from those early days when you all lived on the continent of ancient Lemuria; together you knew how to create and nourish your creations from within a state of balance. You are therefore granted the right to take part in this workshop in which you will return to energetic balance. In a condition of energetic balance, you will connect to your soul purpose. Indeed, these are growing pains because, as your insight deepens, your understanding of your life path becomes clearer and clearer.

Pay attention to what your game is, what role you have decided to play on the only planet of choice, and how you shape the marvelous and wonderful game of your life. Isn't it so? Create this game with awareness, by choice and by divine will. We bless you for your being; you are loved and enveloped in infinite love. Dance with the pink flame of love and the blue flame of divine-will. Charge your bodies and allow the transformation that is created when these two flames are joined. Make your way to ascension at all the levels in which you exist today on Planet Earth, the spiritual and the material, the high and the low. Find the balance.

Bless you, in peace, Adama

The Temple of Sexual Energy

Phase 1: Light Balloon

Let's take a deep breath. Now we exhale, let go of all our thoughts and feel that our body is released. You see a bright ray of white light coming from the center of the universe, from the great central sun. Descending into this room, it splits and goes through the crown down into the crystal brain, where it cleanses the brain of all dark and negative thoughts, leaving it totally clear and clean, filled with bright white light.

The ray continues down into the heart chakra, which opens and expands, filling with bright white light. Our expanded heart fills with love, the love of creation, which comes especially to you, embracing, flowing, softening, until the entire heart is filled with infinite, shining love. The white light continues through our bodies filling them with light, down into the earth. From our base chakra, we now see a thick brown root running deep into Mother Earth to ground us.

At the center of the room now, you see a beautiful energetic portal opening. You are invited to enter, and as you do so, your light bodies pass between dimensions. You see yourselves in an open field, filled with colorful flowers and beautiful trees. The sky is clear and the sun is pleasant. A beautiful figure approaches and greets us, telling us that we have arrived in the light city Telos through the portal between dimensions. We follow him down a path of crystal stones, descending lower and lower until we arrive at a large crystal pool of pleasant, warm water. You are invited to enter the pool and immerse yourselves three times in the purifying water. (Allow yourselves a few moments.)

Now you're out of the pool, feeling pure, wrapped in a white robe and following the guide from Telos along a path of crystal stones to the level of the healing temples in the city. You walk past pyramids of many colors and sizes until you arrive at a beautiful violet/pink/blue pyramid, which is very large, smooth, and round. It is an impressive structure. The crystal doors are open and you go through them to enter a room with a bright crystal circle at its center. You are asked to stand at the center of the circle where there is an orange tube-like flame rising right up to the apex of the pyramid. Crystal chairs are arranged around the center; you are asked to sit on one of them.

The orange flame now sends its rays into the center of your sexual chakra. The orange flame penetrates it, giving off a spark that lights up the chakra. This is the resurrection flame. Your sexual chakra is now loaded with electrons and protons that shine, and as the energy begins to turn, the chakra opens gradually like a beautiful flower made of many petals. You can feel the entire area being rebuilt and recreated, healed and filled with vital energy—life energy, the energy of creation full of passion. See how the chakra is shining now in shades of orange and gold.

Giving thanks for this opening, you rise from the crystal chair. Now you see the guide taking you to another dome-shaped room. In the center of this room, you see blue and pink flames rising higher and higher, merging with one another, and you are standing inside a shaft of light. Take a deep breath. Now you are beginning to feel the dominant energy that exists in your physical light body. Is it blue male energy or pink female energy? Feel the energy very carefully, and when you feel the flames co-mingling, begin to balance your body's energy between the male and the female, until you feel that all your energy is centered, equally contained in the blue and the pink flames. When you enter the beam of light, both the blue and the pink flame move through each of your energy centers, one chakra after the other; if one energy feels more dominant, please ask it to soften somewhat to allow the second energy to enter and create a balance.

Pink energy, the female energy, brings compassion, love, tenderness, softness, intimacy, and flexibility. Blue energy, the male energy, brings focus, leadership, action, control, and sometimes competitiveness. Now see that your bodies are balanced between these two energies, like the two flames dancing together, the female and the male. When you feel that your bodies are balanced, please say aloud, "I am in balance."

Again, the guide from the light city Telos appears and you follow him to another room with a huge dome, in which there are many large balls of light, like transparent light balloons or bubbles. While in this room, you are about to meet an energetic being you know. You are invited to enter one of the transparent light balloons. Now that you are inside, many light beings enter the room, some of whom are present in your life in a physical human body, and others who are not. You see this special being or figure entering the light balloon where you are, and from a distance, you already feel new energy. You may feel great joy, happiness, and excitement in your heart, for you know and are familiar with this light being. Feel the energy of the being standing in front of you, and explore this being with the feeling in your heart. The heart is the source of measurement and understanding, and it is examining whether or not the energy before you is balanced in terms of its male and female energies. Take a few moments. If the being is not balanced, ask her/him to balance their own male and female energies.

Now ask the energy before you whether or not she/he is willing to join you in the process of sanctification of sexual energy. If the answer is yes, you can begin sending a ray of soft pink light from your sacred heart into the sacred heart of this light being. If the answer is no, the being will simply disappear. The ray continues passing lovingly to the light being before you, and you receive a ray of love from her/his into your sacred heart. Now the first soul connection is established and the process begins. While continuing to maintain an energetic connection with your light bodies in the consciousness of the fifth dimension, slowly take in a deep breath and reconnect with your physical body. Open your eyes; in this silence, you will awaken to the here and now and begin moving your arms and legs.

Now we will take a short break and move directly to Phase 2.

Phase 2: Sanctification with the Light Entity

You are now filled with a shining white light. Your energetic and etheric body is reconnected with your form present within the light balloon in the temple of sexual energy. Sense and feel your being present in the light bubble where the energetic being stands before you, and continue to send a gentle frequency of love, and receive a pink ray of infinite love.

Take a deep breath and exhale.

Now, ask the being again if she/he is in balance. If not, it is time for her to balance herself.

Feel within yourself. Are you in balance? If not, it is time to balance yourself.

At this moment, a golden flame emerges from deep in the earth and enters the light balloon. Rising up, it splits into two streams of light rays. One ray enters you through your base chakra, which it illuminates with a golden light; through the ray you enter the base chakra of the light being facing you, illuminating it with golden light. The base chakra opens and is filled with protons and electrons, the particles of the golden flame. The energy continues rising into your sexual chakra and into that of the light being before you. Here too is a golden light illuminating and opening area, and the beautiful flower is filled with shades of gold, rich in protons and electrons. You may feel subtle currents of energy.

The flame continues within you and within the light being facing you, rising into the solar chakra center, filling the seat of the emotions with the golden flame. This creates a form like the two overlapping triangles of the Star of David, one on top of the other, becoming a beautiful rotating energy happening within you and within your counterpart at the same time. The flame rises until it reaches the heart chakra. Entering the sacred diamond, it illuminates it with a beautiful golden light, washing the diamond and filling it with infinite love. The ray flows in the form of the symbol of infinity inside the sacred diamond heart. The flame now reaches the throat chakra, spiraling up and cleansing the throat chakra in a circular motion. You can now make a sound from your throat "Ahhh ....." (Please make your own sound now.) You can see the flower of life manifested, opening the throat chakra gateway.

Now the golden flame continues rising to the third eye, where it sends the golden light through a filter and shines it out like a flashlight, illuminating the whole world above you. It continues up to the crown chakra, and you can see the lotus flower opening. The golden light bursts out through the light balloon where you and the light being are, and fills the entire room with golden light.

Beautiful priests and priestesses now enter the room, dressed in gold. The light bubbles dissolve and disappear, and the light being remains standing by your side. A priest and a priestess come to you and place a beautiful necklace around your neck and around the neck of the light being next to you. You thank the being by your side telepathically.

You ask her whether she wants to continue the process and undergo the energy initiation with you. If she says no, it is time to say goodbye.

You are separating from the light being now, even if she/he says yes, since you will meet again soon. You are again part of the group, being asked to gather and express thanks for the experience you have had. You are all glowing with golden light, charged with sexual energy, balanced and open to a life of passion, creativity, and fulfillment. Stepping out of the room, you see your guide from Telos who leads you to the exit from the temple. You are asked during the coming week to balance your male and female energies (blue/pink), and hold on to the powerful frequency that has entered all your energy centers. You are escorted out through the crystal doors. You see a beautiful oak tree, and are asked to sit beneath it for grounding. You feel the ground. You can lie on the ground surrounded by grass and beautiful flowers. When you are seated, Adama comes to you to bless you give you this message:

Welcome, dear ones. I am High Priest of Telos, Adama, congratulating you on the wonderful work you have done. You must understand that today you have made a quantum leap in energy, in alignment with your intention and according to the vision and the initiation that you have chosen to take on as part of your light path. We are aware that faith guides you in walking this path, but, because your sight is cloaked, your steps must be guided by your sacred heart if you are to find the most accurate answers and feel once again the Lemurian frequency from Telos. We are happy and praise your courage, your will, and your boldness in reaching out and advancing step by step. May abundance and light embrace you. Know that you are loved.

The work you have done today has brought great joy and happiness to the light city Telos, because you are loved as the first light group to come to the temple of sexual energy and undergo an initiation here. This initiation will lead to and open many doors of light, so you must ask yourselves in full integrity and love, "Do I take responsibility for proceeding to the next step?" The answer will burst from your heart in an outpouring of light, love, and excitement from the new opening in your light bodies. From within your physical, emotional, and mental bodies, your being grows and expands with light to illuminate the entire universe. Although your human mind is limited in its ability to comprehend this, the entire universe is illuminated by attunement to the kind of energetic work you have performed today from your sacred heart, as your bodies opened and your light began to shine.

Thus, as human beings you know that you must protect and preserve this place that you have created and are excited to see today. As human beings, you know how to protect and work with those same frequencies and energies in order to maintain contact with the energetic being with whom you became friends today. We are with you; you are not alone. Your being is surrounded by angels, priestesses and light guardians who protect you. In the coming week, observe your behavior, your growth, and your speech; watch to see with whom you meet and socialize. Be aware!

Be aware!

I bestow upon you the blessing of light, the blessing of abundance, the blessing of all that is.

Look inside your sacred hearts and preserve the golden flame frequency that you received and celebrated today. Bless you, and goodbye. Adama.

You are wearing the crystal necklace you received which will keep and protect you in the coming week whenever you feel your energy ebbing. Please put your right hand on your neck and sense the crystal necklace you are wearing; this energy will restore your balance completely. Repeat aloud after me, "Whenever I lose my energetic balance, I feel the crystal necklace balancing, fulfilling, expanding, remembering, and showing me the golden flame within me." Now take a deep breath and remember you need only put your right hand on your neck and everything will work itself out. There is no need to remember the words verbatim since your energy is already balanced in the moment. Everything is manifest in the current moment.

You again see the guide from Telos, and you follow him up to the beautiful golden carriage. As you step inside, the carriage fills with bright white light and we rise and connect to the shaft of yellow light taking us out of Mt. Shasta at the speed of light. We turn east and arrive in the Middle East, coming down into this room. We are now fully connected to our physical bodies. Slowly we move our arms and legs, taking a deep breath and saying three times, "I Am That I Am."

Moving on now to the last phase: the union.

Meditation for the Temple of Union

Dear ones, you are invited to the Temple of Union.

Close your eyes and see yourselves walking along a path of crystal stones that leads you deep into the healing space of the light city Telos. Notice the crystals at the edges of the path; they are of colors you have never seen before. These crystal stones raise the frequencies in your body. Breathe deeply. With every step you take, you enter deeper into the healing energy. You see before you temples of pyramid shape in different colors. A guide from the light city Telos greets you and invites you to move forward with him.

You pass by a beautiful stream and see before you the Temple of Union, whose color is purplish pink. You are invited to enter. You breathe deeply and go in. In the center of the temple, on the crystal floor, there is an illuminated circle. You are asked to stand in the center of the circle, and as you stand in the center, you begin to feel your body being charged with energy. The energy enters all the energy centers in your body and fills them with color. Note which color floods your body, and feel the energy accompanying you. Do you feel male energy or female energy?

Take a deep breath. You are beginning to feel the type of energy that creates balance. Note that an additional energy is now entering the circle. What color is it? Is it male or female energy? Is it in balance? Your energetic image is undergoing a personal balancing; the circle sends the frequencies of balance that pass through all the chakra centers, beginning with the base chakra, to the kundalini, solar plexus, heart, throat, and third eye chakras and continuing on to the divine connection.

Now you can feel the area of the heart chakra expanding and filling with vibrations of love, containing all the particles of the energetic body. You can feel your body expanding and growing and filling with joy and excitement; the frequency increases, and the light bodies expand. When you feel the time has come for union, let yourself feel your bodies uniting with one another and combining in a spiral embrace, energy of one being joining with the energy of another. Note that the connections happen gradually, from the base and solar plexus chakras to connection with the heart chakra.

Take a deep breath, dear ones; feel the shared love and the flame of creation joining your beings. The vibrations of love radiate beyond the pyramid, its spark visible from afar. The activation of the union has begun. The joining of souls happens on a deep level with the souls you have chosen. The energy continues rising through the remaining chakras and connects with the center of creation. Take a deep breath, feel the love, feel the union, and support each other. You can also communicate telepathically. The male energy connects with the female energy and takes on a new hue, a new color of union. Feel the serenity and the quiet; you are charged with all you need in order to continue to bring wholeness to your beings.

Connection with the twin soul energy is thrilling every time. Take with you the memory of the entire process; the union that has occurred remains in the memory of the cells of your etheric body, and it will trickle into the memory of your physical body so that you can act in your world in harmony and in balance between the energetic aspects. The energy of the union brings balance, serenity, and calm. Bless you, dear ones.

Paul the Venetian

The Temple of Union Meditation: the Last Step

You can see a white ray of light entering this room from the center of the universe and the great central sun, splitting into thin rays to enter the center of the crown chakra. We are bathed by a soft, gentle white ray, which passes into our crystalline brain and charges all the cells with cosmic energy, while removing the pressure and thoughts that do not serve us any longer. Now take a deep breath and release it. The ray continues down to the heart chakra, filling the sacred heart with a bright white light. We note how the heart chakra is expanding, and all compressed energy is being removed as we release anger, and perhaps sadness, and the heart is filled with the love of creation.

 The light continues down, washing all the bodies and passing through the feet to Mother Earth. From the base chakra, a thick brown root now extends, connecting us deeply to Mother Earth for grounding. Now you see that in the center of the room, an energetic portal has opened between dimensions, and with our light bodies, we enter the portal. Before us stretches a beautiful field, with rainbows and flowers in a variety of colors we have never seen before. As we enter the field, we feel the wind caressing us and the sun overhead is warm and comforting; singing birds and colorful butterflies are everywhere. Calm and peaceful, we now see a large rainbow in the sky ahead of us, and as we pass under its arch, we are bathed in the colored lights of the seven sacred flames.

Take a deep breath.

We are calm and peaceful and a guide from Telos greets us and invites us to follow him to the temple of sexual energy. We go inside this beautiful temple, built in the form of a great pyramid and connected to crystalline circuits, with beautiful crystal structures colored pink and blue. Standing at the center of the pyramid, we see a bright orange flame. Around us, crystal chairs are arranged in a circle, and we are asked to be seated in the crystalline circuit.

We sit and the golden orange flame sends a ray straight to our sexual chakra. We feel how the ray enters us, extending, expanding, and opening the area. The ray continues, rising higher and higher, and flowing to the solar chakra, which it illuminates and opens with the frequency of life. The golden orange flame rises higher still, until it reaches the heart chakra, which it illuminates and activates with vital life energy. The energy continues upward, a beautiful golden orange flame reaching now to the throat chakra, opening the energy center there. Now we can make a sound, "Ahhh ....." The creativity and creation center also opens. The ray moves upward to the third eye creating an opening, and then continues up and out through the crown chakra. The ray rises until it is connected to the creator, to our higher selves, and to the flame of the resurrection, which is the energy of life.

Let's take a deep breath. We can feel that all the cells in our bodies are open and flowing from the bottom up. Our avatar bodies are now ready for the energetic balancing. We get up from the crystal chairs and follow our guide into a beautiful, round, domed room, where we see shafts of light above us. When we enter the light, it envelops us in both flames, the masculine blue and the feminine pink. The two flames rise from the depths of Mother Earth up through our bodies, and with the dance between the two, create inside us a balance between male and female sexual energies.

Let's take a few moments to focus on ourselves. Make sure that a balance has been created between the blue and pink flames. Talk to the flames if necessary, enhancing or lowering one or the other until you feel totally and completely balanced. When you feel completely balanced, say out loud, "I am balanced." When we feel the balance, we move out of the light shaft and feel as if we are floating.

Already we see our guide from Telos, who invites us to follow him. Looking around we see the beautiful crystalline structures forming ribbed walls of shining crystal. Now we float into a new room, built in the shape of a diamond. Hovering, we reach the exact center of the diamond, and we can see that within all the facets there are other, smaller diamonds that look like private golden rooms. We are each invited to enter a golden diamond. When you have done so, feel yourself inside your personal diamond, note its color and the temperature inside. You are inside this diamond as an energetic being, all your energy centers are open, and the blue and pink flames are balanced. Now, from your sacred heart you invite into your personal diamond, the light being who represents your cosmic partner, your cosmic love. I do the same, inviting the light being who is my cosmic partner. You have invited, from your sacred heart, your cosmic partner in love. Take a deep breath and let him/her in.

Allow yourself to laugh, cry, or feel any sensation that comes to you.

When the energy of the cosmic female or male being is before you, from the bottom of your personal diamond, two golden threads emerge; one enters the channel of your prana and the other enters the energy channel of the being before you. Look now at the energetic being in front of you. Welcome her/him. Now begins the process of unification, the merger between you and the energetic cosmic being who stands before you. These golden threads intertwine you and your cosmic partner, rising up through your sexual centers to the solar chakras and finally reaching your sacred heart. The merging and connection are now established.

Feel now how your heart opens and how the love and light creates a connection between your two shining hearts. As the threads pass from one to the other, the ray of light creates a large circle of light, connecting and uniting our hearts. Let's take a deep breath. As the light increases, a vibration is established between the two sacred heart centers and the light continues to expand.

Moving upward and connecting with the throat and the third eye chakras, the golden threads unite in the crown chakra. They rise, a perfect union, and a great light emerges from the crown chakra centers. We are united as one! There now exists a perfect connection with your cosmic partner, with cosmic energy, as the two bodies unite together energetically into one! Let's pause for a moment to feel this magical union together. You may also receive a higher message right now. Take a deep breath. The connection we have created in these moments with the cosmic energy will support us and be with us, helping us to exist in the fifth dimension. This energy will support us even at lower dimensions, including the third dimension. We thank this energy for the privilege of experiencing together this energetic connection in unity.

Now we ask our cosmic partner to gradually leave us. Take a deep breath, then another, and a third. Now exhale. Disconnection is taking place. The light being is leaving the diamond, lovingly separating from you. At this point an etheric connection is created that will remain in the golden thread so that you can telepathically communicate with this energy, consulting with and receiving messages. Now that you are alone in the diamond, you again feel gratitude for the privilege of this experience; the diamond opens and you are outside it.

We gather together as a group. In the room, we see lights of many beautiful colors and fireworks and great joy and happiness. Rose petals fall from the sky in celebration of the union we have undergone. We sit, calm and peaceful, as beautiful priestesses enter the room and place lovely laurel crowns on our heads. We are filled with joy and excitement as the great masters enter the room with light in their hearts. They bless and embrace us. We are asked to sit on the laurel leaves, and the high priest Adama arrives in the room. He sits down before us on a beautiful crystal chair, and delivers a message:

Welcome, beautiful light group. What a day of celebration this is. You have experienced and been recharged by the light from a solar sun entity, which came especially for you, in order to join your soul in love. This fine love, pure and gentle, you felt in your heart, with ancient longing for the same soul that entered this life with you, a cosmic soul that some of you have not seen or met in many incarnations. But today was a moment when you were connected to the light that helped you to see your innermost vision coming from your sacred heart. With the love for the ancient memory of that special being that joined with you, you created a unity and a great light of infinite love with which you arrived on the planet. This is the love from the ancient creator and from God with which you descended and which you remembered today. This is a wonderful gift that you have given to yourselves; your cells, your memory, your DNA, and your codes. You will take this wonderful gift forward with you in your hearts, on and on and on.

We who feel your development and growth are so happy on this day in which you have decided to follow the path of light with absolute trust, in this exciting human experience. This experience connects you with that which is beyond the veil, to the light that arrives from the higher worlds and universes. With this feeling of oneness, you create the energy with which you can open the planet to a new world and in which you can create differently. Indeed, you understand, dear ones, you have the ability to unite with that ancient cosmic being who arrived especially for you today, in a union of love wholeness. From out of the whole, you go out into your world, and create and live in joy because wholeness is everything.

Wholeness includes within it components and particles that you sometimes do not understand; so when you feel separateness, return to the feeling of wholeness. When you feel a human emotion that leads you to a low place, envelop yourselves with the whole and feel the light flowing in your veins and your cells and helices and codes. Light is the language and light is the speaker, and it is light that floods those places in which you walk today as light bodies on the planet—because you are whole.

Indeed, the features of harmony are the features love, and the features of love are the features of color, and color floods all of creation. This is the new landscape that will be created. Do you see it? Do you see in your imagination that this is becoming reality? Do you see the creation materializing and being realized as you shape it and create it? Does this wisdom exist in your sight, dear ones? Dance the dance, dance the waltz, dance the dance of sharing, dance the dance that gives you the stability for this life. This stability is present within you, and this stability is what shows you where to go. You are like the flowers roses. When you want plenty in your lives, keep the roses beside you, dear ones. Keep them in your hearts. Smell these roses when you want love, and listen to the sounds, the sounds of love which are everywhere in your world. We bless you on this day. We are joyful and happy about the great light that has emerged from your sacred hearts and the quantum leap you have made, each and every one of you here in this room today. Bless you and farewell, you are beloved.

   Adama

Rose petals in many colors and shades are now falling on us from the sky. We walk toward a large gate that opens before us. This gate takes us to a beautiful place in nature, among flowers and trees, where beautiful animals come to greet us. Friends from the light city Telos also arrive to bless and embrace us for the process we have undergone. We see a beautiful carriage before us; we know that it is time to go and that we are invited to visit Telos any time we wish. When we are all inside the carriage, it closes and fills with a bright white light. Up and up we go, joining the shaft of yellow light until we leave Mt. Shasta and head east to reach this room. Now take a deep breath. Begin to move your arms and legs, and say aloud three times, "I Am That I Am."

The Crystal City

I awaken at 4:00 a.m. and am asked to sit down and write. With great excitement for the process, I accept an invitation to enter the Crystal Light City of Telos in the eighth dimension, above Mount Shasta. This first meeting is dedicated to building the light body in the Hall of Creation in the Crystal City of Telos in the eighth dimension.

This is Adama, the High Priest of Telos, welcoming you.

Dear beloveds, you who walk the path of ascension are connected to the highest levels of your soul. Feeling the frequency of Lemuria emanating from the depths of your soul awakens the creation codes. Back in the ancient days of Lemuria, the days of memories and of love, we invite you to join the crystal frequency glow of the eighth dimension. The Crystal City, which was built in a decade in planetary time, now opens for visiting by human beings. The Crystal City above Mount Shasta carries within it the gentle glowing crystal composed of light frequencies and divine heavenly energy particles descending from the central sun, which is the source of All That Is.

We invite you to connect with your etheric body and

accompany us to the crystal flame in Telos in the fifth dimension, and from there to enter the celestial Crystal City. Breathe deeply, beloved ones. See yourselves crossing the multidimensional gateway to the city of light. Here you are in your crystalline body, standing in front of a pyramid, which is a delicate network of crystal light. The pyramid is huge, and the light coming from it is soft crystal light. You are invited inside. Inside the pyramid, I invite you to stand around the entrance gate to the crystal light city of Telos. Stand within one of the circles of light that is coming out of the ground. Breathe deeply. Feel the immense light filling your being and the Creator energy filling your body frequency. Divine love enters your heart, which opens like a rose into the light of God. Feel your crystalline light body expanding. Breathe deeply. Feel the lightness and the love. Now, beloved ones, you are invited to enter the elevator that will take you to the crystalline light city of Telos in the eighth dimension.

The elevator fills with glowing light, rising higher and higher, changing to the frequency of the eighth dimension as it rises. Feel your body light and airy. Breathe deeply. The elevator opens and a bright shining light welcomes you. The City Angel greets you and welcomes you to the eighth dimension. You are invited to leave the elevator.

I, High Priest Adama, am accompanying you, beloved ones.

The city of light in this dimension was built over a decade ago. In the last decade, it has gradually been opening to humans who wish to visit us. We are going from the elevator into a round structure built of triangles. It is a soft crystal structure. You are invited to the Hall of Creation. The doors of the hall open and we go inside. The hall is built of crystal invisible in the third dimension. A gentle frequency of love envelops the place. At the center of the huge hall, a pillar of bright white light can be seen. Around it is a circle of running water, but the water is not compressed, as we know it. Made of crystal, it flows quietly. We are invited to sit in crystal chairs.

We are about to create our crystalline body, refined by the crystal and the new cell memory of the eighth dimension. Each of us is sitting on a crystal chair. You can see and feel the soft hologram frequency of the crystalline grid surrounding our etheric body and the crystal body that already exists. The crystalline grid is assimilated into the body of the crystal and refines the frequency of the light. The crystals that contain the body become refined. Every cell opens and undergoes a frequency transformation into the eighth dimension. Breathe deeply. The crystal body carries subtle codes with which we can "cruise" freely in this city of light in the eighth dimension. Breathing deeply, we already feel the airiness, gentleness, and lightness of our bodies. Beloved ones, in your existence in the frequency of love, your body becomes refined, your diet changes, your speech and influence reverberate across the planet.

As more and more human beings transmute their frequency, Mother Earth ascends.

We in the light city Telos have embraced the frequency of the eighth dimension. Today there are a number of light cities in the eighth dimension open to human beings. These light cities fulfill different roles. The work in this dimension is done on the soul body, after the emotional, etheric, and mental bodies have been healed and the frequency in these bodies has risen.

It is time to look at the soul, which, having connected with the "I AM" presence, carries within it the doorway to divinity. In these light cities, there are temples and study centers that focus on the soul. It is possible to look into all aspects of the soul in the parallel dimensions you have chosen to experience for your spiritual development. Breathe deeply and feel. Get to know the crystalline light body. The body maintains within it your familiar energy centers with its DNA codes. You are invited to stand up and float in your crystalline light body. Feel your being. You have transformed yourself into a light being. You are invited to move with your light body on a journey in the beautiful city.

Leaving the Hall of Creation, we continue to float inside a beam of beautiful light that takes us into a huge pyramid of delicate lilac-colored light, soft and inviting. The lilac pyramid is performing a delicate transformation of your energy. You are invited to sit around the delicate lilac flame. Observe and feel the flame. See the sparks coming out of it and entering your body as if forms. Breathe in all the light particles that are being assimilated into your body. This is your delicate crystalline light body. Feel the love saturating you with a soft light and continued expansion. Breathe deeply. We are entering the room of the angels, who bear a delicate liquid crystal drink that appears like vapor. You are invited to drink or inhale it deep into your body. The crystal drink contains tiny balls of light and positive ions that infuse your body with the gentlest of electrical pulses to strengthen the body. Drink and breathe deeply.

Indeed, you have a new body. We welcome you to the process that you continue to go through. Breathe deeply. The angels of the flame monitor and support the formation process you are undergoing. You feel the flow of the frequencies entering your body. Breathe deeply and feel the expansion. Look at your body. Do you see its form, with its many colors and contours? Notice lightened density and the feeling of levitation. Breathe deeply. Indeed your body is ready to go to the crystal city. You are invited to accompany me. Beloved ones, float along with me. We are leaving the pyramid of the lilac flame. We feel the ease of floating. The light beings of the city come to meet us. They welcome you in peace, congratulating you on the forming of your crystalline body. This is the body with which you will enter and deepen your visit to the Telosian light city in the eighth dimension.

The city sprawls above Mount Shasta and beyond. In the city, there are learning and treatment centers linked to even higher dimensions. The residents of the city and the city council in each dimension manage the city independently. There are many angels and celestial light beings in the city, which have come from distant galaxies to study and deepen their knowledge of Planet Earth. We bless you, beloved ones, for being celestial beings capable of transmuting and creating this exquisite crystal body that is adapting to the frequencies of the eighth dimension. Your body will form slowly and will absorb more and more frequencies from this dimension. The more you visit the city of light in the eighth dimension, the more effectively you will begin to experience your higher soul.

I congratulate you on your journey of light and ascension. I bless you, beloved ones,

Adama

Part IV

The Journey of Ascension

We call upon you to choose a life of community action, a life of action for the sake of others, and of seeing the radiance of your soul. When you learn to give of your sacred heart and to maintain emotional, physical, and spiritual balance, then you will reach ascension.

The Game of Enlightenment: the Stage of Ascension

Dear ones, this is Adama. You are witnessing the approach of the time of entry of the new energy, which is arriving from the source of the One, from the source of the center of the universes, from creation. Indeed, the energy entering the planet is being refined and as it enters your light bodies, your etheric bodies, and your physical bodies, your enlightened bodies undergo a transmutation in a process you are directing.

Therefore, the existence of human beings who are pursuing awareness and containment of the light in the physical body is expanding, and will continue to expand with the absorption of this energy and its vibration; whereas those who are not on the path of awareness and light will be unable to contain this sacred energy.

Dear ones, the only star of choice grants you the right to choose the time of your awakening. Indeed, precious souls who are dormant will awaken at later stages, but we yearn for an awakening among a high percentage of humanity. The souls who do not awaken at this time will choose again to continue playing the game of creation. The planet is moving into the phase of ascension, but it will not happen in a single day. The transition is multi-phased and multi-dimensional. You must understand that thought processes are changing and will become, along with all that is familiar to you, unessential in the higher dimensions. Thus, your brain is awakening at this time to new patterns of thought. The new children on the planet are already familiar with these patterns and work accordingly in various situations, but the world of adults awakening to the light at this time are being exposed to these patterns of thought gradually.

This is why you are noticing so many workshops, lectures, and meetings on the subject of enlightenment and each person connects to the frequency right for itself in a different way. Every soul that awakens connects to the vibration that is right for it and to the soul family with which it arrived on the planet. There are many nuclei of souls, and you are attracted to one another like magnets.

Dear ones, these are Messianic times and we are glad for the great awakening of the sons and daughters of Lemuria, a group whose role in the process of ascension is most important because they have taken upon themselves the responsibility for enlightenment. They and the Pleiades were among the first light entities who arrived by choice in order to take a central role in the divine game of creation whose influence is felt today. At this time, we, the sons of Lemuria and the Pleiadians, are reconnecting to the planet in order to conclude this final stage and the excitement is great. Yes, dear ones, you who read these pages feel, remember, and know that these are the facts, and that this is the truth, the answer to all the confusing questions that are arising. We bless you, dear ones, for opening your hearts, for the opportunity you are giving yourselves to reconnect to the vibration of Lemuria. We bless you for your desire to remember and take a conscious part in this game of enlightenment and this stage of ascension.

Dear ones, the change you are awaiting, but of which you are fearful, is approaching. The date 12/12/2012 is the date the Maya foresaw, the date known to many as the end of one energetic era and the beginning of a new frequency entering the planet. In this period, there will be many new discoveries. Crystals have always been important for the planet and many more crystals will be come to light. Historical findings will be revealed that will alter the understanding of science and the face of history as you know it. Continents will move and Mother Earth will change. Indeed, the change is taking place. This change is part of the energetic planetary transformation Mother Earth is undergoing, as are you, dear ones.

Don't cultivate fears in your hearts. Understand that the sons of light who are on the journey of enlightenment and are establishing a direct connection to the higher self and the sacred heart know where to be at the right moment. Indeed, a certain percentage of the population will be kept safe. Those who are not connected to the ancient way and longing for the light, whose eyes are closed and who adhere to the third dimension—which causes human beings to behave out of fear, ego, control, and force—will have to continue their incarnations on other stars intended for that purpose. You must understand that I have no wish to arouse panic or anxiety. Quite the contrary. Understand, dear ones, that these are the days of choice on the only star of choice. Many of the sons of light who are illuminating the planet will help during the early stages of awakening to transition to the next stage, the stage of ascension. However, the sons of darkness, in whose souls the spirit of darkness prevails, will be forced to leave.

Dear ones, the planet will ascend into a phase of harmony and love and peace. Yes, loved ones, only those who can bear the frequency of love will stay and live in light, awareness, and happiness. These are the days that are approaching for the entire planet. We, the light entities, the masters and the angels who support and accompany you out of love for you and out of the desire to help you with the process, are glad for these days. We have undertaken to be at your side when you awaken and extend our hands in blessing. We whisper in your ear, caress your hand, and walk with you through the phases of awakening toward ascension. Indeed, dear ones, in all the light cities, we see how human beings are awakening. Many exalted beings have said that humans are in such deep slumber that they will miss the designated date. But, dear ones, human beings are up to the galactic task. Many, even more than are required for the mission, are awakening these days. A large portion of humanity is undergoing a rapid change, a transformation supported by the violet flame and Master Saint Germain. The entire planet is bathed in the violet light of transformation, which accelerates the protons and electrons in your bodies and makes you feel, sense, remember, and ask questions on the universal level to carry out changes in the way of life familiar to you. We are proud of you, dear ones.

In the past, the beloved light entity Aurelia Louise Jones transmitted messages about our light city Telos, about our way of life and the way we understand the way of light in the frequency of love. We continue to disseminate, from within the great Telos community, the light of the heart frequency, and thus assist Lemurians to reawaken to the new energy on the planet. Indeed, more and more Lemurians are awakening at this time. Telos organizations around the world are transmitting the soft frequency that comes from the heart of Telos. This frequency is spreading, reaching many, and touching many, and we are happy that Lemurians are returning home. With each son of light who awakens to his Lemurian heart, we too in Telos are enlightened. Your being comes to us by night and by day, performing deep healing and cleansing. We are with you on the path of your personal enlightenment. We see how you meet each other and realize that you know each other from the earliest times. You engage together in many activities, spreading this loving frequency, and in this way enlighten more and more sons of light.

We are happy and Telos is celebrating. Telos is expanding these days. We are making preparations in the mountain and beyond in additional places for our population and the sons of light who reach us. Indeed, Telos today is a light city that has expanded greatly since its inception.

I now invite you to close your eyes, breathe deeply, and see before you the rainbow. You are walking along a path of colorful crystal stones, a path that leads you to the center of the light city Telos. The fountain stands before you, illuminating and sparkling, and the eternal flame shines at its center, rising up.

Look around and see that you are here together with sons of the light city Telos who greet you with a blessing of love. Breathe deeply and feel your sacred heart opening and expanding to the frequency of love. See the children of Telos coming to give you a blessing of peace and presenting you with roses in all the colors of the rainbow. See the crystal buildings beside vegetation that is unlike anything you have ever seen. See your loved ones at your side. The light city blesses you as you enter Telos. You are invited to continue your tour of the temples of healing of the seven flames, temples that invite you to enter and embark upon a fascinating journey, a journey of healing all the levels of your etheric, emotional, and mental bodies in the Lemurian frequency of love that will return you home. Breathe deeply.

The Acceleration of Time

Dear ones, we are accelerating time. The magnetic polarization familiar to you in recent centuries has changed, and its shift influences the acceleration of linear time as you know it. During the day, the accelerated tempo can be felt at the physical level and that is why you tire so often.

You must understand that your physical bodies are undergoing changes, which you may or may not be aware of, in order to adapt to the new energies. Although there are regions in which a significant change has not yet occurred, by 2012 the entire planet will have undergone changes.

Mother Earth is being reborn and shifting in the poles is being manifested at this time. Continents are moving, as are the seasons. The climate is changing and temperatures are rising. These are only some of the physical changes happening on the planet. The spiritual changes are even greater. Human beings are waking up at this time to a new vibration, asking questions about the essence of life and the existence of the soul, about the essence of energies and the connection to God. Humanity is awakening.

From Telos, we are watching the amazing process you are carrying out, dear ones. The work of distributing the light is being done, and the new frequencies are reaching human hearts. These are the frequencies of ancient Lemuria which existed in vibrations of love, of giving, of sharing and of brotherhood. Life on the planet was a life of consciousness and sublime happiness. Today, after many years of waiting, we are transmitting to you the results of in-depth research we have done in Telos over the years. We are working with you and accompanying you through the physical changes you are experiencing in opening the heart chakra. We are with you, hand in hand, instructing you, guiding you, encouraging you, and awaiting the reunion. The reunion will take place when we are able to leave Telos and you are able to enter freely and visit the light cities. That time is nearing.

We encourage you to come visit our temples to experience healing within the magical flames that are an expression of divine will, and to make possible the rapid growth of your souls. We come to you in your dreams to assist your souls to remember the steps that bring you closer to being connected anew to your home. Indeed, dear ones, we encourage you to awaken. From the city center, we watch the stars that envelop you and caress your body, and the angels who whisper in your ear. We are witness to your awakening. These are days of joy in Telos, on the planet, in this universe and in neighboring universes, and in the heart of the Creator. These are sacred days. Continue on your path and awaken to your sacred heart.

Planetary Changes

Telos has grown and expanded during the years of its existence as a light city, and we have developed a life of light beneath the surface. The light city of today was known to a few people in former times, enabling their development while waiting for the right moment for change to begin. Indeed, in Telos, there exist more than a million light entities working to rehabilitate the planet and cooperating with the sons of the earth who are connecting with their Lemurian heart. The city is built of many parallel levels, and continues to grow. You must understand that we live in the fifth dimension, making use of the inner space of the volcano, Mt. Shasta. But understand too that it is possible for us to continue deeper into Mother Earth and the region around the mountain. We are not the only ones. Light cities all over the planet are growing and expanding rapidly.

The study of geology known today is incorrect for the most part. There are spaces in the earth's crust, and not all the mantle is full of burning magma. Throughout the planet, there exist spaces and immense crystal caves that have not yet been discovered. On the planet, there exist additional reservoirs of water that have not yet been revealed to humans. There are also reserves of natural resources whose location we do not wish to reveal, so that they will not be exploited by the forces of darkness. We are safeguarding these resources for the future existence of humanity.

At present, Mother Earth is cleansing herself of the filth, with the help of sons of light who work with us who are fighting to clean up the planet. There is an awakening and an awareness of the entity called "Mother Earth." The crystals that were implanted in the distant past are awakening at this time; they are connecting with the crystal grid that surrounds the planet, and in this way, a direct connection to the creator is made. The energies being absorbed in your body are also being absorbed in Mother Earth, and are helping her to ascend. The climate of the planet is changing; the period of warming will lead to a period of cold and a great deal of precipitation and this will change the climate as you know it. There will be floods and climatic regions will change. The cyclicality of the planet will continue. In the past, humanity was not always aware of the need for changes in earth cycles and was wiped out as a result. It is important to note that this time, these shifts will be made in complete awareness and harmony with human beings. Information will arrive in time; many humans will have to relocate, places that were deserts will become green, and fertile areas will undergo a process of stagnation.

Dear ones, of course this process is a long one in the eyes of the observer and the reader. You are invited to imagine, with the eyes of your sacred heart, life on the planet awakened to beautiful days, days of climatic balance, days of cleanliness and plenty, days of renewal of nature and of life, days of flowering.

We walk hand in hand on the only star of choice, in the awareness of a world that runs entirely through harmony, giving, compassion, and love.

Dear ones, I am with you wherever you wish.

Adama

Message from the Light Entity Gabrielo about Planetary Changes

Greetings, I am Gabrielo, a light entity from the fifth dimension, who has been walking in the light city Telos for some thirty thousand years.

Dear ones, the foundation of the city with its many levels and vegetation of nature beneath the surface, were done by me and my partners on the journey. We did this through precise planning and magical creation. When we arrived at Mt. Shasta, the mountain was desolate. First, we were asked to perform energetic purification. The place contained crystal caves, but it was necessary to recharge them with the energy of creation. After a few years, we managed to produce the light energy from within the crystal caves that we needed to sow plant species and varieties brought from our mother stars.

With the arrival of the mother ship Mu, light entities from our home arrived and brought more seeds for planting. We planned carefully which species would be part of our new home, and so it was. We planted tropical and Mediterranean trees, trees that grow in the desert and many plant varieties unknown to you. In the gardens, you see flowers of countless colors, some of which you have never seen. The vegetation today includes thousands of species and varieties and we have transferred some to other light cities. Thus, we created our gardens, something that would have been impossible without the crystals, and we thank Mother Earth for them. The vegetation that exists today on the planet is undergoing a transformation; many varieties have become extinct, but new ones are growing in places, such as in the Himalayan Mountains, where new varieties are growing in the crevices among the rocks.

Your scientists do not understand the meaning of this phenomenon, but in the coming decades, the matter will be studied. We invite you to visit the magical garden in Telos, to walk through it and learn. We ask those of you who feel your purpose is to preserve different kinds of flora on the planet to come to us to study, learn, and volunteer. Join organizations that preserve the forests and the gardens, and receive anew the knowledge of nurturing and preserving living things. This knowledge is available today. We are waiting for you, dear ones, waiting for you to awaken and begin to take responsibility for the plant life of the planet. We are transmitting the knowledge and codes on this subject to the children and youth of Telos who wish to make this their profession. Light entities from Telos will connect with all whose hearts are open to this frequency.

We are with you in the journey of ascension. Blessings of light and love.

Change in the Frequency of Mother Earth

Dear ones, at this time the changes we have been awaiting are happening throughout the planet, and from Telos we are witness to the transformation that is happening. We have been operating from Telos for tens of thousands of years. After the sinking of ancient Lemuria, we arrived on the planet of our own free will with the intention of continuing the Lemurian mission and disseminating Lemurian vibrations. We did this by means of an experiment. In this experiment, we volunteered to play according to the new rules of free choice, because the creator saw in them a meaningful lesson for all the souls that would come to this planet and to all the universes and stars that would observe it. The significance of free choice in this game is that every soul undergoes the lessons it has chosen in advance.

Thus, we descended, at first connected to our higher consciousness, but later "falling" from higher consciousness to a dark place that had no connection with the divine source, a place in which some of you, to our regret, still exist. These are Messianic times. You are awakening, the crystals are awakening, and various light groups are fulfilling many roles needed for awakening to come about. Many light entities are enveloping the planet so that the processes that belong to the Age of Aquarius will continue at an accelerated pace. We in Telos and other light cities on the planet and in other universes are watching, we see the new state Mother Earth is entering, a state of healing through light and through the heart, and we are glad of this. This is the mission you are carrying out, dear ones, and we are with you, walking with you on the journey of awakening, while Mother Earth prepares herself to absorb the vast new frequencies of this era.

In the course of this journey, you are witnessing many changes about which we have already spoken. Some animals will complete their existence here and will disappear, and new, unfamiliar animals will arrive in their place. The role of the dolphins and whales, for example, who arrived on the planet long ago to carry the frequency of balance, is about to end. At this time, many of you human beings are connecting to the energies of marine animals and are drawing from them the knowledge relevant to your continued growth. The light entities familiar to you as dolphins and whales are returning to their planets, some to the star of the Lemurians, some to the Pleiades, and some to other stars less familiar to you. The oceans are also undergoing significant change, as the composition and structure of the water is changing. Some of the oceans have lost their balance because of high levels of pollution; others are undergoing a process of restoration and cleaning, a process that will last tens of thousands of years; and still others are shifting with the displacement of the earth's crust. This is also why many marine animals will become extinct; but, with these changes, new configurations of the water and the animals will develop.

In certain places, there are crystals planted in the ocean depths that are beginning to awaken after many years of inactivity. The cooperation between sons of light who are above ground and sons of light who are deep in the earth is beginning to happen, as guardians of the crystals meet with light entities situated above ground and transmit information to them.

These are Messianic times, and we are with you. We invite you to enter our temples in the various light cities and disseminate the information you receive. Your physical body is undergoing change. Accept these changes and seek the support of the many communities interested in maintaining a clean body. We congratulate you on your activity and accompany you every single moment in your new reality. Remember that the journey is shared, and that we are with you. Enter your sacred heart and ask questions. Connect with the vibration of love through which you are awakening. Let yourselves feel, breathe, and live in this vibration.

I bless you on this day of celebration.

Adama

Temple of the Dolphins

On the flora and fauna level in Telos, there exists a beautiful temple built of a unique crystal. The temple covers some seventy acres of earth and contains pure, pristine sea water. Its floor is made of different crystals that raise the frequency within. This is the temple of the dolphins. The temple of the dolphins was built especially to enable ancient animals familiar to you, such as dolphins and whales, to exist in a frequency above that which exists in earth's oceans. Your planet, which received these wonderful animals, has undergone significant changes over tens of thousands of years during which the original composition of the oceans has changed. For the marine animals that inhabited them in the past, it is difficult to preserve a high frequency these days, and is the reason some of marine animals are choosing to leave the planet. Thus, you are witnessing many incidents of dolphins and whales suicidally beaching themselves.

    The planet today is performing energetic cleansing. In Telos, we have chosen to preserve these kinds of marine animals, so we have presented this temple to a few dolphin and whale families. In the temple, they are able to preserve the clean, pristine frequency in which they arrived on the planet. These animals are rich in knowledge. They activate ninety-five per cent of their brains, and they have wonderful communication and transmission abilities. Their knowledge resides in their DNA and contains codes that have been preserved through the ages. Their transmissions often reach us, the sons of Telos. On many occasions, we come to the temple of the dolphins for healing and balancing our frequencies, and when we swim with the dolphins and whales, we are able to provide healing to places in need.

Meditation with the Dolphins

We invite you to breathe deeply and fill your body with the light ray of the turquoise flame. You see yourselves in a carriage full of bright white light, and in it, you take-off up into the sky. The carriage flies at the speed of light and connects with a beam of yellow light descending from the center of the divine source to Mt. Shasta. The carriage enters deep into Telos, where you get out and follow a guide from the light city. You walk along a path made of crystal bricks that leads to the level of the animals. You see before you various temples, among them a turquoise temple so enormous that you cannot see where it ends.

As you follow the guide, a large crystal door opens; you enter and come to a small room. Through the transparent crystal, you can make out a gigantic aquarium filled with clear sea water. This is the home of the dolphins of Telos.

A family of dolphins approaches and invites you to swim with them. You accept the invitation and at once notice a one-sided passage through which you can enter the world of the dolphins. You enter and find yourselves in the water, breathing with no difficulty through the crown chakra.

The dolphins connect with you, greet you, and invite you to hold on to them. You communicate telepathically. Each of you grasps a different dolphin, and you begin a shared journey. The dolphins take you deep inside, into the depths of their temple. You see before you sparkling crystals and continue sailing inward, until you reach a circular center in which there are crystals of different kinds and sizes. The dolphin brings you to a specific crystal, whose frequency is identical to yours. You hold the crystal while the dolphin scans your body with his special abilities, allowing him to see all your inner parts. As he scans and finds places that have energetic blockages, he asks the crystal to send light rays to those places, and you feel your body expanding and opening.

Feel how every single cell in your body is breathing, expanding, becoming enlightened, and opening to the frequency of creation. The crystal continues its work and you feel support and love.

The dolphin continues to communicate with you telepathically. He may advise you what to focus on at this stage of your personal journey, or how to deal with a person who is close to you. The dolphins are ancient friends; each of you feels that there exists a deep familiarity between you and the dolphin who is accompanying you. You are each invited to ask the dolphin's name. Your time is up. The dolphins take you back up to the entrance; the turquoise color stays with you throughout the process. You feel pure, calm, serene, joyous, and loved, and you know with inner certainty that at any stage you will be able to connect again with the dolphins.

You go into the small sealed crystal room and from there leave the temple, enter the carriage full of bright white light, and begin to rise. Connecting with the beam of yellow light, you depart the city. You leave Mt. Shasta and return to your homes.

From Theory to Practice

Adama, what must we do in order to turn good will into action that leads to change?

Good will is like a good deed. Therefore, dear ones, when your intention is to contribute in a positive and constructive way, your actions carry the frequency of the love of the fifth dimension you are experiencing. When you return from the fifth dimension with a positive charge, the physical body connects with the etheric body and receives that positive charge and you illuminate your surroundings with your light. The light affects your body, your mood, your positive thinking, and so forth. As long as you remain in a state of positive charge, your cosmic synchronization is precise and you have the ability to create. On the other hand, when you come into contact with light bodies whose charge is negative, the negative charge penetrates your body and your balance is upset. There is a decline in enlightenment and a drop in energy, and every drop brings blockages, fears, and the creation of negative reality. The vision you are so close to achieving again recedes.

Therefore, dear ones, we recommend that you safeguard your energies and avoid meeting with human beings who bring you down. We recommend that you practice meditation every day so that in your renewed contact with the fifth dimension, you will be able to maintain an enlightened light body in which positive protons and atoms flow. That way, when you next meet bodies who do not have a high frequency, your light will succeed in maintaining balance. When you are in contact with negative light bodies, and a human being directs negative energy at you with words or deeds, this can have long-term effects and can even cause damage to your physical body. This is the reason, dear ones, that you may no longer associate with those who were once your close friends. With the purification of your light bodies, you meet new friends, sons of light who support you and accompany you on your path to ascension.

We are with you, breathing, caring for, and healing you when you come to the temples of Telos to be healed and energetically replenished. Indeed, this year an immense and magical portal has opened to humanity, a portal that welcomes your choice to connect and to awaken to your sacred heart, the heart of creation, the heart that contains within it particles of life that have chosen to awaken. Yes, dear ones, this is the hour when you awaken to a profound consciousness that gathers within it the deep levels of memory from ancient times, from the days of Lemuria. These times that are reawakening. At this time, we are in greater need than ever of enlightened consciousness. We need more than ever the renewed connection of your being with your consciousness.

The spiritual being connected to your physical body creates the reality we wish to maintain on Planet Earth. You are awakening to a life of harmony with a desire to live in a world that sees the light in every action and in every creation, a world that breathes the love in every step and in every connection.

What should I do with the knowledge, and how can I develop from it?

The knowledge that you acquire awakens, stimulates, and arouses your body and your soul. Furthermore, dear ones, words carry a frequency, albeit an invisible frequency but one that is felt, that arouses the light body and creates enlightenment as you read the messages. Therefore, channeling that does not come from a clean place is liable to bring you down energetically. Understand that you must take the role of the channel seriously, because it is significant. The channel must prepare the bodies before the channeling with pure intention, and must transmit the channeling without bringing in his human aspect. When the knowledge comes to you, it is pure and its purity can be felt. Thus, channeling can awaken and enlighten as you progress on your personal path of enlightenment. Sometimes a channeling directs you and connects you with another human being you have met seemingly by coincidence—but it is no coincidence. Your frequency attracts everyone who vibrates with a frequency similar to yours. Of course, the meetings from which you learn in depth were determined long ago, at the time when an overview of your present life was planned.

Adama, how can we implement in the third dimension what we feel in our heart in the fifth dimension?

Well, these insights of yours are now being tested and these are the insights you must implement. The rules of the fifth dimension can be applied in the third dimension. You are familiar with the laws of creation and with the tools given to you, now is the time to consciously apply these laws to your behavior as human beings. Your thoughts create reality. That is not a slogan. That is the way things happen. Your words create your being and the feelings of your heart fulfill your dreams. Look to see how your behavior changes the reality around you. See your world balance when you are balanced in your sacred heart, and use the tools we are giving you to remember to balance your bodies.

Take care to meet with each other in community and provide emotional support for one another. These are the important things, dear ones. Human society is facing change, the change that comes with enlightenment and a new understanding. We appeal to you from Telos and from other light cities all around the world, to choose to live a life of activity for the good of the community, and to see the brilliance of your soul. When you learn to give of your sacred heart and to live in emotional, physical, and spiritual balance, then ascension will exist.

We are aware of your way of life and the physical hardship you have to cope with. We see your material world and the superfluous consumption in your society. Change the way things are one. Do you really need all the physical objects that exist in your physical world? Look around and see which objects really serve you and which do not.

Your society is awakening. Create within it a new reality. Don't give the giant corporations that control the population of the planet the power to continue directing your lives. You lead, dear ones, lead from the light and the truth. Write, talk, meet, and discuss shared ideas in love and your life will change. New patterns are forming and new thoughts are being created; it is time to use them for action in your new lives.

We are with you, blessing you. We are with you, feeling you. We are with you, supporting you. Feel us, hear us whispering in your ears, and see us smiling. We are at your side in your personal journey, your group journey, and the journey of humanity into enlightenment.

The Changes in Our Bodies

Dear ones, the sons of Telos and I, Adama, welcome you and invite you to the healing aspects of the city. In the healing activities, there are unique treatment centers where you can find all seven flames that can be used to help perform your daily work. Each of the flames has a unique quality according to its special hue. They enter each of your bodies—the etheric body, the spiritual body, the mental body, the emotional, and also the physical body—to work on the protons and electrons, the cells, the DNA and all those living particles that make up your body. You must understand that we in Telos perform healing every day and work with the flames in the temples, because in the fifth dimension, too, light work is essential for the healing of the body. Although our bodies are not dense like yours, we too sometimes sustain a condition of imbalance; hence, we make sure that healing is part of our lives, rather than waiting for a painful condition to develop. We also follow a refined diet. When a light body becomes unbalanced, it affects the environment of the sons of light close to it, and we have a great sense of responsibility for fellow beings.

Dear ones, you are not so different from us. The sons of light who work with refined energies influence their surroundings; the light one gives off does not remain only in one's physical and etheric body, but is disseminated over distances and touches the hearts of your dear ones. This is why it is so important for light work to be done in each and every home. The Sabbath candles traditionally lit in the Jewish religion distribute light in all the homes.

We see that today most of those engaged in healing therapies are women. The priestesses are awakening, women are again leading, and women are transmitting enlightenment to their children and partners. The spirit of feminine energy continues and will continue to grow stronger as the light is disseminated on the planet. We are glad of this. We have known times of love, harmony, and compassion arising from feminine energy on this planet.

Men, too, have a very important role in these times, but we will not discuss it here.

You must understand how your body works and breathes. You must remember how to work with the body, how to think and feel from inside and how to properly use the brain, because many organs in your body are only partially active. When the light breaks through the limits of science, scientists will understand that their eyes have been closed up to now, so that when they receive information, they will once again act in accordance with the laws of the fifth dimension. When that happens, there will be a different awareness regarding nutrition and the functioning of the body. The way of life will change and your body with all its parts will undergo a rapid change in order to be ready for the fifth dimension. Among the light workers, there are human beings who are at present preparing their bodies with our guidance. They will continue to live in the third dimension, although they will have the ability to pass completely into the fifth dimension. This is already happening, but it has not yet been revealed to the masses.

You must understand that the awareness is spreading, light is filling every corner, and in time, humanity will understand. We too undergo a change when, in our meetings with you, we adapt ourselves to your vibrations and learn how to reach you most easily. Indeed, the descent is most challenging, because the density in the third dimension is great; however, that is about to change. Understand that you are in a stage of learning, of awakening and of gaining experience. Listen carefully, dear ones. We accompany you in your dreams, in astral meetings, in meditation and even in daily life.

Joining the Light Bodies

Telos is one of many light cities that have existed for ages on Planet Earth. Many of you have read and heard about it. We are witness to your visits to Telos by night in your sleep. At that time, your light bodies connect to the consciousness of the fifth dimension to perform healing and to meet with your families, with your light bodies in Telos, and with the masters.

Sleep is one of the tools for sustaining life in the physical body, and those hours give your souls what they need to continue to exist, to develop, and to grow. The nocturnal meetings are vital to your spiritual development and growth. In the morning hours, with the connection to your physical, spiritual, mental, and emotional body, you connect with a frequency that is important, even essential, to your continued existence. Dear ones, you must understand that the times in which you are living at present are accelerated, and in order to advance your spiritual growth, you must access on a daily basis a conscious connection to the energy of the creation, the higher self, your "I AM" presence. We also recommend that you connect with Telos with an awareness of your longing to be joined with your families, the temples, and the flames and healing practices. This energetic balance vital for you.

When your being is in a state of full consciousness and energetic connection to the fifth dimension, the change you are undergoing is manifested in all the bodies—the physical, the etheric, the emotional, the spiritual and the mental. The work you are doing in the temples with the healing flames on your etheric body simultaneously influences all your other bodies. In this way, a connection among the bodies is created and imbalance is prevented. When the bodies are connected, you can gradually continue to ascension.

Your parallel bodies must be balanced and identical in frequency, color, sound, and resonance. Yes, indeed. The bodies were formed together and they contain all of these qualities. You came into the world with all the bodies, but sometimes, when you are faced with the "veil" of reality in the third dimension, disparities form between the bodies. These days, when you consciously reach the healing temples of Telos, you are beginning to restore balance and reconnect the bodies, and thus are able to move forward to the next stage in the initiation. With the joining of the bodies, your spiritual being expands and gains in power. We see and feel this and can encourage you to connect further to your parallel selves, which exist in parallel dimensions, near and far. Most of you, dear ones, who are rejoining the Lemurian frequency, have a dimensional form in one of the light cities on the planet, for example Telos, in Machu Picchu in South America or in another light city.

With the connection to your presence in a light city, you will be able to unite with the light form and be assimilated into it, thus joining a powerful frequency that contains the most ancient knowledge that has existed since your creation. Remember that this light form is not the only one; parallel with it, in parallel universes, there exist additional forms of your being. Your being is energy expanding beyond time and space, beyond what exists and is visible, beyond all human understanding. With spiritual growth, the connections to your being become clearer to you and you become aware of more detailed information. Your physical body can contain a more powerful frequency, which raises the body to the frequency of the fifth and sixth dimensions, and even beyond. Your body, now able to contain these powerful frequencies, connects to its entire being with all its strata.

Thus, dear ones, you are rising through the stages of initiation toward ascension. The existence of the masters who have ascended and united with their bodies is at such a high level that they do not need a number of bodies; hence, they have released their physical, emotional, mental, and spiritual bodies. These bodies have not disappeared, but continue to exist at a different energetic density. At this time, as we are awakening to the One, awakening to cooperation with you, beloved human beings, we extend to you the knowledge with great love. We invite you to Telos and to all the light cities on the planet in order to continue the work of healing and rejoining of your bodies. We are with you, accompanying you, supporting you, and embracing you.

Meditation: Connecting the Bodies

Take a deep breath and see how a white ray of light enters deep into your physical body through the crown chakra. Breathe deeply. The ray is illuminating your physical body and washing away all that is superfluous in your physical, etheric, emotional, mental, and spiritual bodies. It continues down through your feet and from there goes out into Mother Earth. At this moment, a beautiful carriage is taking shape around you. You sit down at its center and the carriage fills with bright light and begins to move. It rises high into the sky, and with the speed of light, turns west. It hovers over continents and oceans and flows into at a beam of yellow light, descending into Telos in Mt. Shasta.

The carriage comes to a stop. Now it opens and you get out. You are welcomed by a guide from Telos, who invites you to follow him down a meandering path made of beautiful crystal bricks, lined by crystals of different colors and tones. As you walk along, you see an enormous rainbow of many colors, and when you pass under it, you see before you crystal pools carved deep into the crystal rock, each pool a different color. You each choose a pool and immerse yourself in it three times. Note the color of the pool you have chosen. With each immersion, you clean all your bodies and revitalize them. The water purifies and penetrates all of your bodies and fills them with the life energy of Creation.

Now you feel light and calm. You get out of the pool, wrap yourselves in a white robe, and again see the guide from the city. You approach him and he takes you to a spiral crystal staircase. You go down the stairs until you reach a large room made of crystal. At the center of the room are crystal chairs, and you are invited to seat yourselves on them. Under each chair is a spiral of a certain color, and as you each sit on your chair, the chair begins to rotate in a spiral movement. The floor rotates in a spiral and you feel your bodies rotating together. As the bodies rotate, a ray of a certain color is sent from the center of the spiral, and its color penetrates all your energy centers. With every slow, circular movement, your bodies join one another. Take a deep breath. You can feel the etheric body joining with the other bodies—the emotional, mental, spiritual, and physical. See how all the bodies become a shared being, expanding and filling with bright light with every rotation. The being continues to expand and grow. Breathe deeply.

When the chair stops moving, you arise from it and give thanks for the process you have undergone. The guide leads you to the spiral staircase. You ascend and go out to the carriage. You have the clear knowledge that you will return here very soon. You get into the carriage and it rises higher and higher, connecting again with the yellow beam of light, and continuing to rise leaves Telos.

The Stages in the Journey of Awakening

Dear ones, we are continuing to transmit knowledge to you human beings who have chosen to awaken, to change your body, to raise your vibrations and to take part in the rebirth of Mother Earth. The knowledge that arises today is arriving from many light entities in the fifth, sixth, and seventh dimensions, and even higher. Some of you are being exposed to knowledge from extraterrestrials coming to fulfill their role on the planet at this time.

Your body is awakening, first of all, from the activation of the DNA helix, and then from daily meditation. During meditation, dormant places in the brain awaken. These are areas that were awake in ancient times but have fallen asleep, and all that's needed is a new spark to awaken them. In every meditation, the pineal gland once again begins to absorb the particles of light flowing to it, and in this way, the divine connection is formed. The other parts of the human body undergo changes after you work on all your energy centers. Every center awakens and washes away former lives until it reaches a pure state; at that time, the physical body begins to change its shape.

Have you noticed that you are waking up in the middle of the night? Have you noticed that you are eating different foods than you did previously? Have you noticed that you are sensitive to an unbalanced environment? Are you cutting down on alcohol consumption and giving up cigarettes?

In every transitional period, as your body undergoes changes, supporting angels are helping you to pass more easily through the stage of renewal. This stage may last months or even years, depending on your seriousness and determination. We are accompanying you during the process. Some of you are beginning to develop vision in your third eye and others are developing their hearing, their sense of touch, or their sense of smell. The awakening body is connecting energetically with the grids that surround the planet. For the most part, this happens after the physical body has completed the cleansing process.

Have you noticed that you were thinking about someone and then suddenly bumped into them? Have you met someone and noticed you both felt the same sensation?

Indeed, your telepathic sense is awakening and being restored, allowing you to enter gradually into a way of life that is not yet quite in the fifth dimension, but is no longer the way familiar to you from the third dimension. We are in a period of transition, and we must create a bridge to transmit knowledge from the fifth dimension to the third dimension in which you live. In the next stage of awakening, knowledge begins to arise in you. You are beginning to open to light entities from the fifth dimension and receive information from them. This is a fascinating stage; you will feel like a child tasting cold, sweet ice cream for the first time and you will delight in your creations. You are aware of magical action and be able to feel how magic works. Thus, dear ones, you continue to spread your light by means of creativity and action.

At this point, some of you may fall victim to the ego; sometimes there may be regression. Even in this case, if there is a part of you that continues to rise in pure love and divine will, connecting to the light and to love without the deceptive ego, you will be able to be achieve full connection with The One, a connection that will stir your heart.

You shed a tear and feel the peace. We are with you, moving on with the mission, continuing to guide you in cooperation. We see the stages you are passing through, and support and accompany you so that you will arrive safely at an enlightened place from whence you will spread the light through your heart. We are proud of you. We are happy with the steps you are taking and with your choices. We are with you. We are one. Continue experiencing the unique era that is illuminating the planet.

Dear ones, the meaning of working from the heart is to think and feel your surroundings through your heart. When you choose this way, you operate in a different manner; the flow feels perfect and the result is positive. In your world in the third dimension, there still exist many who act out of personal interest. This energy originates in a person's lack of balance, creating many dramas in your lives. You must understand that when people are charged with negative energy, they are charged for only a few short moments. After this, they return to a vacuum where there is neither drama nor excitement. Such people find it difficult to achieve balance. Balance is important because it leads to calm and harmony in your environment; harmony leads you to connection with the whole, and to the hearts of those around you. With such energy, many beautiful things are created. You must understand that in a place that is unbalanced, the particles of life are distorted, so you feel weak, angry, and unloved. There is a desire for love as compensation, but when love comes from the wrong place, the compensation is short-lived.

We are noticing a phenomenon of eating sweets; people eat sweet things in order to compensate for deprivation. This is an illusion. The sweetness calms the brain for a few moments, but before long the body returns to a state that may be even more unpleasant when surplus sugar in the body causes imbalance. Take care, then, to be in balance and to find out what is good for you. Try to live in a supportive environment; work in a place where you create with passion and feel fulfilled; choose a partner who empowers and strengthens you; and bring up your children in joy. Maintain all the goals to which you aspire. Connection to the light empowers these intentions and reduces imbalance.

Connection with your soul will make you act in a conscious manner and maintain what is positive in your life, living in love and through choice at any given moment. Remember that the awakening is connection to the light in all areas of life. It is the awareness of the here and now. It is the place from which you can create the reality of life in the fifth dimension. To have this awareness is your choice.

Accompanying you on your journey to the light, the High Priest, Adama.

Activating DNA

Let us take a deep breath. We are seated in a carriage and it rises upward. The carriage connects with a beam of yellow light that descends from the center of the universe and begins to descend with us to Telos. The carriage opens. We are received by a guide from Telos. We walk behind him on a meandering path of glimmering crystal lined by large crystals of various shapes and colors, and come to a large cavern in which there are more crystals. We enter it and stand in a circle. At the center, the crystals disperse their light throughout the space. We now watch a sound-and-light show held especially in our honor.

Above each of us is a large, unique crystal and we begin to introduce into our etheric bodies the colors of its rays.

The pink ray enters and colors the body and the chakras, filling the whole body with the energy of love. Let's take a deep breath and feel it permeating all the particles in our body, every proton and every electron.

The yellow ray, the ray of knowledge and enlightenment, begins to wash and color the entire body, and we can feel the cells awakening and connecting to the ancient knowledge hidden within us, knowledge that will deepen with time and guide us on our way.

The blue ray is the ray of divine will. Each of us connects to our higher self, to the Creator. We have chosen this journey, and our higher soul has chosen to develop at an accelerated rate, which we have been experiencing in recent months, that will lead to the enlightenment of humanity and to raising our vibration.

The green ray enters us, permeating all the deepest strata of the etheric, emotional, and physical bodies and healing every area that is still blocked and in need of treatment.

The orange ray is the ray of revival. We fill all our bodies with this ray, through which we see our purpose in lives in this Messianic age.

The white ray includes within it all the rays. This is the ray of ascension, which enters deep into our bodies.

The violet ray enters and is helping with our transformation at this very moment.

Our body is ready for the next activity. Following the guide, we go deeper into the crystal cave until we reach another dome. The walls here are covered in a gold color. We are invited to sit in a circle on crystal chairs. We shall now do some serious work with our DNA to absorb energies from Mother Earth. While working with the crystals, we have done internal work on personal spiritual growth, work that has led each of us to the place we are today. However, we have not yet realized our full potential. To this end, we are given the possibility to activate our DNA. We will be happy to expand from two DNA helices to twelve, then to thirty-six. Within the helices, we will activate our memories, gifts, and skills.

We will now each look into our etheric body. We look inward and see the two helices of DNA connected by a central axis and colored in different hues and shades. To the two helices, we add two more of different colors; they connect at the same spot, and all the helices rotate on their axes. Each helix rotates independently. We now add two more helices. Let us breathe deeply and see the spiral movement of the helices. We will each say to ourselves, in pure intention, the following sentence:

I take it upon myself to open up to the helices of DNA that have been created and are anchored in my physical body, in my etheric body and in my light body. I am open to receive information from the codes and I am open to the changes that will take place in the coming days. I am open at the highest level of my soul. I encompass the energy of the codes found in DNA at present in this Messianic era.

During the coming week the codes will continue to rotate on their axis, and each of us, in keeping with our personal growth, will receive information and will be charged with energy appropriate to our personal development.

Now a golden ray arrives from the dome of the cavern above, and enters the crown chakra of each of us. The DNA helices continue to rotate and will continue to work throughout the present life and help us with the mission.

We remain seated on the crystal chairs, about to receive a message:

Rules of the Light Disseminator

Greetings dear ones, this is Adama.

The combination of the flame of rebirth with the flame of transformation is an essential combination at this time. These are the two flames that will bring about immediate changes in the hearts of light entities, both for those at the highest levels who have already opened to the light, as well as for those in the third dimension who are about to open to the light. Work with these two flames is essential to the process Mother Earth is dealing with. Support for her energetic shift will help contain the intense energies that are entering from the central sun that must be absorbed by the earth and by the physical bodies of human beings.

The Middle East region continues to undergo changes at the physical-geological level. Many energies have entered recently through the existing portals in the area and have been absorbed into the sacred earth. Your work with light energy helps the energies be absorbed without causing serious geological changes. The Syrian-African fault is active, and were it not for the light work, the earth of the region would be shaking and erupting at this time. Because many light entities are located in and above your region and light work is being done every day, it is possible to balance the energy and help Mother Earth to contain the intense new energy that is entering this area.

The region is undergoing great change within the human beings. They feel in their sacred hearts that peace is the only possibility for existence in the area. There is no way forward aside from peace, brotherhood, harmony, and the vibration of love among the local peoples. Indeed, that is how it will be. New leaders will arise soon, on both sides, and will sweep the peoples in new directions. New ideas will appear that will lead to renewed choice. We are working with you towards this shared goal.

At the national level, you must perform several tasks in order to help raise the vibrations:

1. You must insist on working daily with the flames, because this energy is important to the process of treating your physical, etheric, and emotional bodies. The daily work allows you to be in a balanced state and prevents you from falling into the drama. Only from a balanced state will you be able to perform your light work in the best way possible.
2. You must meet once a week as a group of more than two people to consciously aim to raise the vibrations in the region, to heal anger, to heal the human hearts that are still dormant, and to appeal to the higher self of many light entities. Through this work, light will be sent to those people whose higher selves have already opened, but who are having difficulty connecting to the light body in the third dimension. You must send your

light so that it will reach all who are meant to awaken.

3. You must observe life through the eyes of a master with love for the world, and act from the heart, not from ego, control, or fear. Work and observation through the heart are most important; you must connect every morning with your sacred heart.

4. You must maintain a healthy diet, including fruit and vegetables, clean water, nuts, almonds, and protein of animal and vegetable origin. Take care not to eat foods containing artificial materials, processed foods, or foods containing excessive salt or sugar. These materials are liable to cause energetic blockages in the etheric body that will need much time to reopen. It is very important for you to maintain a pure and clean body.

5. You must take care not to become addicted to materials that lower the energetic frequency, such as alcohol, cigarettes, caffeine, and sugar. These addictive substances will distance you from the fifth dimension. We have discussed addiction to cigarettes in one of our earlier books; take care to avoid that habit.

6. Join with the forces of nature, take walks, and work out of doors. Earth opens the dormant chakras, cleaning and purifying them. Listen to Mother Earth and her messages. Go for hikes. Avoid long exposure to electronic devices. Avoid sitting in front of the TV or the computer. These electrical appliances transmit concealed frequencies that have negative effects on your thinking. Go out and liberate your soul.

7. Love yourselves, love your body, love what you do and what is around you. Connect with the emotion of

love several times every day. Wake up with a feeling of gratitude.
8. Be sure to test your vision once a week. Observe your personal global vision through the pink flame and visualize how it is being realized in all its dimensions. Join with it from your heart.
9. Remember that you are not alone on the journey. We are with you—the angels, the fairies, the unicorns, the Lemurian friends throughout the world—we are all one and our purpose is shared. Find a group you can join and receive full support for your path. We love you and are proud of your way of the heart and the light.

Adama and the masters from Telos.

The Human Genome

Dear ones, at this time, we are transmitting a great deal of information to you human beings who are performing light work. The days and the times are changing rapidly and time has accelerated. With this acceleration, activity on the surface of the planet is also changing, and your physical body is reacting with sensitivity and openness to the new vibrations that are entering Mother Earth at this time. You must understand that the change is extensive, applying also to animals and plants. The structure of material is changing, and the level of density is also shifting. Sons of light who are carrying out work daily can feel the difference. They feel the intensification of the vibrations in their bodies and the connection with places that are opening and allowing them to connect with the fifth dimension.

The changes are occurring in all those whose hearts are at one with their souls. This will increase in all those who are interested in taking part in the Lemurian mission of intensifying the vibrations on the planet. Those who take this upon themselves must know that it is a total commitment and that the process is powerful and quick. DNA transmits the signals of the new knowledge to different parts of the body that have been blocked; this window opens and you change. You experience the fifth dimension in astral walks to magical light cities in parallel universes, and in this way, you broaden your imagination and are able to go beyond the accepted borders. With this exposure, your soul receives new insight and thus you grow and expand and rejoin your immense soul.

We, the masters, the priests and the children of Telos, are accompanying you on a quick journey. You are invited to enter the light city revealed at this time as it opens its gates to human beings who have connected with the vibrations of the heart. We and you are one in the Lemurian mission to spread the light.

The human genome has duplications and it has parallel layers. The human genome has never been clear to human beings, but at this time, it is being revealed in a new way that is unfamiliar to you. Scientists are beginning to be aware that it is not linear, but parallel with two or more sides. In fact, you human beings have many genes and physical abilities of which you are unaware and which you have not experienced for a long time. Connect with your soul and you will be able to see beyond the material world and hear in a different way. Connect with your soul and you will be able to change the physicality to which you have been attached for so long.

The times are changing and so are you, dear ones, and it is important to venture into the unfamiliar. We are transmitting knowledge in order to reveal the truth and push aside fear. Children of light are arriving on the planet.

They have a different perspective, which is revealed in their behavior and their body language. The familiar is changing. We are facing new times in which humanity will advance, and with light and love, we will reach the harmony needed on the planet to sustain ourselves.

Strengthening of the Way

Congratulations, dear ones, on your wonderful progress. Your progress is visible from afar. Light that is carried aloft is visible in the most distant places. You, sons of light, are awakening and joining in the work of personal cleansing and purification that is so important. Balance is essential in this new energy that is being transmitted to you. Meetings within the Telos community are also vital to your wellbeing. This is the place to share experiences from the higher dimensions, and this is the place to support one another. This process of rapid growth needs support from above. However, it is important to be attentive and fully integrate your experiences in the light with the physical-etheric-emotional-mental body so that you can again be rooted in the earth, in your reality in the third dimension.

This process is ongoing and active. Remember on a daily basis to breathe in the flame with which you last interacted in meditation. Visit the light city Telos. You are invited to the sixth and seventh levels, and, of course, to the healing level you have already visited many times. The present time affects the continued acceleration of the planet, and every soul that awakens at this time, is important and vital to intensifying the enlightenment of the planet. You must work in cooperation from within your Lemurian hearts. Join with one another and initiate ways of spreading the light in your world. Join the organizations that work with energies from the old world and speak in your language. Be the sons of light that you are. The old organizations will take on a new character and open to new ideas. Those whose hearts are closed will leave the game.

These are Messianic days. In parallel universes and on distant stars, eyes are turned to Planet Earth. We in Telos are working toward a shared goal, in cooperation with light cities on earth, with extraterrestrials from distant planets and with humanity. We congratulate you for your path and for your courage. Breathe the flames into your entire body and drink clean water. We are with you, accompanying you at every step. Dear ones, open your heart and act from there.

Who is the Master?

Greetings, dear ones. This is Adama.

Dear ones, the community framework of the light city Telos includes a group of masters who are responsible for the array of energy of the seven flames. With these flames, the people of Telos and the masters of the flames work and purify themselves every day. They are accompanied by others in the city who volunteer for the job for the sake of the community. These sons of light from the city, who give of their energy, receive all the necessities for their spiritual and family existence from the community. They fulfill this ongoing practical role in order to support the life of the light city and of the planet in a spirit of unconditional and unlimited giving. The way of life in the fifth dimension is different in time and space from the way of life in the third dimension. It is not easy to explain it to you. Understand that the system that directs and supports the light city and light work consists of a council with thirteen members. I, Adama the high priest, run the council by virtue of a high appointment I received from the king and queen as well as an even higher appointment from the Lemurian star. Each of the masters who fulfill a role started out as a teacher who gave of himself. Benevolence and unconditional giving are the guiding principles in every moment throughout the day, everywhere in the light city. There is no expectation of a reward. We are unfamiliar with the remuneration that exists in your world. We do not live in that density.

The masters who have experienced many incarnations in the third dimension and have dealt successfully with control, competitiveness, and of course, with the ego, have graduated to ascension. It is they who have disseminated the energy of love, compassion, giving and sharing. You must understand that a master who is a spiritual teacher, cannot transmit words of light and the energy of the spirit, nor can he touch the hearts and souls of sons of light, if he himself does not act with an open heart, giving unconditionally, with complete faith in the Creator and in absolute obedience to the laws of the cosmos. The role of the master is first to listen, then to be heard, and only after all this, to demand. He must love unconditionally, and guide and instruct with a sense of mission and faith. Thus, light entities reach the rank of master in the fifth dimension. In your world, dear friends, although some human beings have begun the journey in absolute faith and with a heartfelt sense of mission, many have "fallen" because of ego. Many human beings are in an egoistic state. They shout to be noticed and to be at the center.

Dear ones, that is not how to reach the desired state of awareness. Righteous action, teaching and charity are done in secret, as it is written in your scriptures. They are done out of a purity in which there is no ego, and in absolute charity in which there is no expectation of a reward. The master acts from an inner place that sees first of all the other before not himself. Dear ones, many sons of light have fallen because of ego. In order for you to be able to spread the light without being hurt and without falling, you must pay attention to the personal areas that require purity and love from within yourselves. Understand that in Telos, too, we contribute on a purely voluntary basis. Our energies are directed toward the general good—from the whole to the individual. We are all one.

Is every human being who walks the path of enlightenment a worthy person?

That is a question you must ask yourselves, dear ones. At this time, when rapid awakening is made possible, there exist dangers in absorbing the intense light, in opening the codes, in restoring the memories, and in the ability to touch the energy of creation, the energy of being. Sons of light activate the powers of light for the sake of the light, but this can also activate the energies control, aggressiveness, and ego and thereby cause distortion. The light frequency that was clean, becomes unclean. So, you must each ask yourselves many times when the information that comes to you is right for you, and whether the enlightened person standing before you is worthy to lead. Indeed, dear ones, we are often witness to enlightened awakening, but also descend into the low characteristics that exist in the third dimension that are difficult for many of you to shake off. Ego, control, and aggressiveness come disguised as a son of light and can capture many human beings. Many are harmed by a son of light who does not operate at the high frequency to which they aspire. These human beings are blinded by the light, and if they are not attentive to their sacred heart with every step on their path, they are liable to be burned. Therefore, dear ones, be sure to enter your sacred heart and ask yourselves whether or not the person before you is transmitting worthy messages.

You must understand that at this time, the time of mass awakening, there are no more "gurus" to lead the crowd. Nowadays, you are the guides; it is you who are the masters. So look deep inside into the abilities, the faith, and the love within you. Feel your sacred heart and think from within it. In this way, you will be able to feel who is disseminating the light at the right frequency to help your development, and who is in fact acting from ego, control, and aggression. The choice is free. We, the spreaders of the light who are in touch with you, see in the sons of light the ability to be open to us in faith and with the wish to recall the powerful frequency of love. We, working with you in cooperation, transmit knowledge through many channels of light. Some of the knowledge transmitted is interrupted along the way, and some gets through. Sometimes the energy of the human being who is a channel is distorted and the knowledge is transmitted in an unworthy resonance. This happens in cases where the human being who claims to have special channeling powers, is not communicating with light entities but with beings who pretend to be sons of light.

How, then, can we tell the difference?

The answer can be found in your heart. The heart absorbs the frequency of love and feels the frequency that opens the heart chakra. The heart knows and remembers;

the heart chakra recognizes the frequencies of light, and responds with both physical expansion and love energy that grows stronger in the heart chakra. However, when the information contains vibrations of ego and control, the emotional body and the heart recognize these energies. In this way, you can discern between a person who transmits purified messages full of love, and sons of light who transmit messages at frequencies of energy that are distorted. It is important for you to know that the purpose of the pure communications is to share knowledge that develops the ability of human beings to understand the significance of the era and the changes taking place in the areas of human, national, planetary, and cosmic life. The purpose of this flowing knowledge is to raise up, enrich, and teach human beings to change their bodies and to align themselves with the vibration of ascension present today. This is why the knowledge is of such immense importance.

We are all one. Bless you.

Leadership

I bless the light entities paving their new way in this life, the way of light. It is immensely important to disseminate the light in all the institutions in your world in which the old energies still vibrate. There are organizations that operate in a destructive way. They rely on the energies of lies, deceit, corruption, and manipulation. Dear ones, your light work is of immense importance in these places. By means of the right thinking and the new vibrations you disseminate, more human beings will awaken and undergo a significant change in their present lives. The lies appear enormous, but notice that at precisely this time the truth is coming forward into light.

Old organizations will fall and new ones will develop in their place. Even now, the change is evident in the crumbling educational institutions; we see more and more indigo children breaking through and setting up schools where students study by free choice. Indeed, light children are growing up in a suitable place. In the future, more and more systems will fall apart, like your disintegrating health systems. Today, more and more therapists are working with light guides as well as with our friends the extraterrestrials. The change is happening and will accelerate in the coming twenty years. Be prepared for the change and lead it.

These days you are witnessing in your region leadership that is not operating truthfully, and, indeed, it will not remain in power for long. Be prepared for a new leader to arise who will lead you to unite with your neighbors. The new leader will have new energy and the group that supports him will work harmoniously. This unity will come about in a new vibration. Only in this way, can the two peoples, the Jewish and the Ishmaelite, join heart to heart and live in peace and harmony with one another. These days will arrive soon, and you, dear ones, must continue the light work, vibrate through the heart, and disseminate at every moment the long-awaited plan from a place of truth, love, and divine will.

You are the guides, you are our emissaries, and we are your emissaries. The shared work raises the vibrations of love in the region. The crystals have returned to life and the change is happening.

Giving

Peace, dear ones, this is Adama.

I invite you to enter the city of Telos and form an impression of our community life. Life in Telos is different from life in the third dimension because we live only in light bodies, and so we hover. The energy of light entities in Telos is both male and female, and every soul can raise or lower its body's vibrations independently. In this way, we can leave the light city with you and join you on the surface, something we do not do often because our vibrations are quite different from yours. Your bodies do not allow you to raise the vibrations to a higher level. That makes our meetings difficult. Therefore, only a limited number of human beings have been invited to enter. The most convenient place for us to meet with you is when you visit us in your astral body in the fifth dimension.

You must understand that cooperation between us is essential, and that we in Telos work hard to sustain it. Of course, the purpose of life in Telos, first of all, is to continue to maintain the Lemurian essence that chose to come to Planet Earth in order to take part in the game of the

Creator. When the continent of Lemuria sank, some of us reached the city of Telos and built it. Today, our community numbers a few million. We sustain ourselves, and also many other light cities, in the awareness of the changes that have been taking place in recent years. The awakening is great and includes many. The change is rapid and will accelerate. Although not all human beings will awaken, all those whose souls came from ancient Lemuria are awakening at this time and taking part in the Lemurian mission. These are most exciting days. We ask that you proceed in accordance with the vibration of love, and that you perform daily cleansing to prevent falling into lower vibrations. The community in Telos is a supportive community, and we hope that you on the surface will support each other.

We are with you, dear ones. Come to us and connect with the ancient knowledge. Even in the days of ancient Lemuria, community life was cooperative and there was a great deal of giving. We remind you that Planet Earth is the only place where free will exists for each soul, independently. In most universes, entities live as a group, but without giving, a group cannot exist. With the return to the vibration of giving that comes from the source of the sacred heart, we will approach the vibrations of the fifth dimension, and harmony will once again exist in your world. In Telos, each light entity voluntarily performs a function for the benefit of the community. The society is based on the principle of "one" and anyone who is unbalanced harms the whole. Therefore, in order to achieve unification, it is necessary to help and be supportive.

In the various meetings with Adama and the light entities from Telos, the importance of working and giving unconditionally has been brought to your attention, again and again. To you, human beings, who so many times observe the world through your filters, without really feeling those around you, are you aware of others? Are you aware of the society in which you live? Do you take responsibility for the society in which you live? Do you take responsibility for what happens around you? Do you volunteer?

Unity is a significant word these days. From 2014, humanity will unite. Light groups will come together, and the desire to replace the old frequency with a new one will arise from the understanding that we are One, and that there exists an enlightened chain linking us all. When this chain is enlightened, the skies of the universe will be enlightened. Dear ones, enlightenment is immensely important. Each and every one of us is a link in the chain that begins with the first link, with the understanding that the individual is part of a cosmic whole. Therefore, it is important that we learn to accept those who are different from us and to support one another and create cooperation. In this way, we will reach a unification of the whole. We in the city of Telos are with you. We see the changes you are experiencing and we congratulate you for the change you are carrying out at this time, individually in your own life and jointly in your world on Planet Earth.

The Awakening of the Golden Age

Awakening into the radiant consciousness of the heart of humanity, we look back over the events and energetic experiences of the past twelve months. The year following the opening of the immense cosmic portal on 12/21/2013, has been a year of challenges, events and experiences.
So now, what lies ahead for us?
The portal opens, light rays with light frequencies from higher dimensions flood Planet Earth. Gaia is transforming herself. Gaia is transcending. You feel the earthquakes, the climatic and economic changes. You make discoveries that hint at the glorious historical past of humanity. You are aware, observing and asking, "When in the journey of Life is the moment of my enlightenment?" You are supported by the Galactic Council which sends the soldiers of light to fully support humanity—the new humanity. We see the war of light against darkness and the light is accelerating the process of purification in the darkest places. Many organizations are faltering—there is no room for lack of honesty and truth. The light expands human hearts. It arrives and illuminates the divine spark in all levels of humanity.
Are we prepared for the changes coming?

2014—a year of spiritual maturity.

A wonderful time to turn inward, as if entering a cocoon and asking questions. What changed for you in 2013? Where have you demonstrated real change, to yourself or to the human collective since December 21st of 2013? How do you see 2014? What are you creating, feeling or planning? This is a golden age, a time when we sense the flame of rebirth washing every cell, atom, and electron. Do you know how to nourish your entire body with this flame? Do you know how to ignite the divine spark in your existence, in your humanity?

The golden age is a time of choice, arising from spiritual maturity, from responsibility and dedication to the Ten Commandments that reverberate in your DNA. In fulfilling the laws of the fifth dimension, you will grow into consciousness of the light and fulfillment of paradise! Tomorrow when the day grows longer, tomorrow with the light coming in, breathe the light rays of the central sun. Breathe the light rays with every cell of your body and choose.

The celebrations continue, sons of Telos, and the light cities of Planet Earth open their gates, granting you the expanse of timelessness. Grant yourselves multidimensional space and visit us in the fifth dimension. Ask whatever you want to know. Dare to go beyond time and space and human intelligence, which hold you back with the familiar, the conventional. Change your ways of thinking and discover the alchemistic, multidimensional, divine way of existence in these very days. We are accompanying, supporting, and following you attentively on your journey toward ascension.

The Council of Twelve, Telos

Reaching Our Personal Purpose in the Golden age

The Purpose is that part of spirit that comes to Earth with its unique path. Indeed, when the spirit looks again at the force of Creation and prepares its newly created Earthly life, it is aware of all the qualities and all the lessons with which it chooses to deal again after experiencing so many Life incarnations – an additional refinement allowing the spirit to grow and enabling it a spiritual Ascension in its Earthly Life.

Upon your arrival on Earth, forgetfulness befalls upon your spirit, closing your eyes, and once again you probe in darkness, your Soul coming to meet with friends for new learning and growth, playing the game without any Divine connection until your soul chooses it's time to awaken, it's time to break through. Each Light spirit chooses its own time and pace along its Earthly Life toward illumination. Yet, indeed, there are also spirits who do not awaken at all and continue to create for themselves the illusion of Earthly Life even after death and separation from their physical body. There are also those spirits who upon passing the Light Canal reconnect with the Will of God, finding enlightenment once again...

You, my Dear Beloved Ones, have reached a present phase where you are fully awakened. You have chosen out of awareness to grow in Light for the sake of Ascension in this present incarnation of your Earthly Life. And therefore, you have to closely observe your own Purpose of Life. Yet again, you have to remember your choice out of your own connectedness to Divinity, out of your own connectedness to the Creator. Once more from that place where you have the opportunity to choose your course and path in these present times.

Indeed, Dear Ones, the Purpose is the choice where you fulfill your insights and knowledge of all past incarnations in order to implement compassion and creation from within your own Will of God. The spirit finds its role in the Divine game, the game we all play with different roles. In these enlightened times you have the opportunity to increase your creative power, coming from a place of giving, from a place of Love, and in doing so, influence the passage of this planet to a new enlightened world. You have the opportunity to choose your role by entering your sacred heart, the place where the Divine Spark resides. Observe yourselves anew at this point in which you live, a point that will change your personal course, a point that will change your soul and spirit, including those who parallel and surround you. The choice of the Purpose affects the whole spirit – with correct choice of Life in balance and Connectedness to Divinity you raise your whole Spirit, as above so below, thus allowing all your parallels to reach Ascension.

With the fulfillment of its Purpose, the spirit expands and reaches Unity with Creation. Together with Creation, your being, a Divine being, creates all there is out of the void, creating a new human society encompassing all vibrations of Energy that did not exist on this planet for eons of times. You have to remember, dear ones, that your purpose is a breakthrough to enlightening many others and that your personal Purpose is an additional part of the whole.

Indeed these Messiah's times, these accelerated times offer a different meaning from what you have known in the past. Your spirit functions simultaneously in various, parallel planes allowing you to live in the Fifth plane as opposed to the Third. Growth will continue and become even more accelerated. With its fulfillment and the Divine connectedness, your Purpose will fill spaces and gaps that were required to be filled. The challenges will continue to arise in front of you and you must understand that these are the lessons with which you ascend and continue to grow.

Look inside, into your sacred heart and ask from your "I AM" to reveal to your Soul the lessons that need to be learned, to be healed and released.

When you are breathing Divinity, observe, live, breathe, and behave through this Divinity – you are the Master. That's where you are heading, each and every one of you, in your own way.

The fulfillment of the Purpose leads to the goal that was chosen. And the chosen goal, although different, is similar among people of the Light. It is time, beloveds, to reach your new Purpose, a Purpose that helps you become born anew for the sake of its fulfillment. In these days, while connecting with your families, your memories, your codes, you touch Creation, and your work as creator is so important in our worlds. Your mission is so great.

We are with you, following you in every way. We see, hear, touch, and caress you. Continue your growth. Work in co-operation, giving from your Lemurian hearts out of Love. Yours, Adama.

11 Steps for Finding the Purpose

1. Write a list of your talents, fields of interest, and innate gifts (that you can or cannot benefit from). Write about one that you wish to develop.

2. What are the things that you like to do when you have time? What do you enjoy doing?

3. What are the things that you see others do and wish to also do in due time? What can be the "perfect" job or career for you?

4. Write of a significant spiritual experience you've had and how it has affected your life?

5. What do you think or feel of that will make the family, the community, or the world a better place?

6. Write the most exciting future that you can imagine for yourself.

7. Make a list of lessons that you've experienced several times in your life. Write about those that are still in process.

8. What can you teach those who are just one-step behind you and who pass the same challenges?

9. Which compliments do you get? Use your imagination. Explore the ways in which these qualities can empower you?

10. What childhood patterns of behavior do NOT serve you anymore and still continue to exist in your adult life? See how, with the release of these patters, you heal yourself.

11. Pray, meditate, ask God, a spiritual teacher, a guide, an angel or a wise man, to give you insights related to your spiritual goal. See, hear, or feel answers that correlate with you. Also, write down insights, dreams, daydreams, etc...

Part V

The Code for Peace

A gentle frequency of love, a gentle frequency of harmony and unity—this is what is needed in order for peace to exist in the Middle East.

***

Dear sons of light, dear Lemurian entities, I am transmitting additional content at a level of vibration different from the usual, through the light entity Ayelet. This content is intended for all those who perform light work beginning from the present incarnation at any given moment.

Light work is performed in the third dimension and it demands the investment of a great deal of time and energy. The codes will be revealed only to those light entities who act with self-awareness and spiritual awareness every single second of their lives. You must understand that the codes are accessible to all, to all sons of light; but even among sons of light, there are those who are unable to be a hundred per cent of the time in the fifth dimension. There are light entities who manage to split themselves and be in the third dimension and the fifth dimension simultaneously. The third dimension is full of presence that draws energy, and because you are in places that upset your energetic balance, your visits in the fifth dimension are essential. You must continue to go there, to be washed, and to raise the vibrations throughout the day.

Indeed, there is work to be done. Therefore, dear ones, we will transmit the codes to you in the course of ten meetings. The code meditations must be held at one-week intervals.

With you, Adama.

The First Code: The Kingdom Chakra

Peace, dear ones. Welcome to the first meeting in which we will give you the information about the codes.

The codes are an ancient source of knowledge, and in the days of ancient Lemuria they were accessible to everyone. The sons of light underwent a process. They were able to pass through ten stages on the path to truth and light and at every stage, they received a certain code with which they existed in the fifth dimension. Entities that went through all ten stages were entitled to appear in the sacred hall, and express their divine wish for life in the fifth dimension and for the main activity in which they wished to engage for their community. Thus, many of the sons of light gave the community their light and received light from their comrades in return. Giving is an energy that empowers and increases the light so there is great importance to this path.

At this time, we are continuing to help you activate the dormant parts of your body via the energy centers, where the central sun is distributed to all the protons and electrons in your physical-etheric body.

Understand, dear ones, that your bodies are nourished by the energy of creation, which reactivates your system of codes. The system of codes is nourished by the energy of the Creator and the information within the DNA helices. The information today is located on twelve helices, and soon they will be multiplied threefold to thirty-six helices. This is the time to open the energy centers.

Today we will hold the first meeting in which we will open a window to the first chakra, the kingship chakra, which has a direct connection to the Creator. We will begin with the highest and move down, although in your world it is the practice to begin at the bottom and move up. The goal is to open up to all the strata of codes hidden within you. The divine connection is the starting point in the journey to the light. The codes transmitted to you with choice are the codes for the direct connection to the Creator, a connection that gives you the ability of absolute choice and the ability of absolute creation.

The high code of the connection to the beginning, to the highest divine source, connects to the blue flame.

Breathe deeply and repeat the following words three times:

"I have loved all the days. I have loved in all times. I have loved all and forever. I AM Love. I AM THAT I AM." These words are said in the halls of the temples by all who engage in light work and the direct connection to the creator. The creator we are referring to is the creator of the present universe who created the planet and created every thought and creation that exists on it.

Connect to the kingship chakra and visualize that you are led to the temple of kingship, while the golden flame burns and rises upward. Feel how you are connecting in the light directly to the creator. Take three deep breaths.

A golden quartz stone is assimilated into the kingship chakra and the code opens within you. Say "Amen." When you have finished, you will be led out of the temple. You are invited to visit at any time from the point of time in which you exist.

The Second Code: The Crown Chakra

The information about the codes is arriving at this time, and it will be revealed so that sons of light working with light will be able to accelerate their spiritual development, reach the high dimensions and combine the light energy from these dimensions in the third dimension, where you are in your physical being.

The second code joins you to the source of the knowledge, which is the source of the light in direct connection to the central sun. The central sun sends rays, and in this way, frequencies rich in information are sent in codes that are being discovered and are opening anew in your etheric body.

We are working with the crown chakra. This chakra absorbs the energy and assimilates the information into the area of intelligence in your physical body.

The region of the brain has grown, and in those sons of light who connect to the energy that enters from the central sun, the brain is undergoing a transformation. The codes open new memories. The brain begins to make use of those areas that have been dormant since ancient times, and it will utilize fifty per cent of these regions, as opposed to the situation today—only five per cent of utilization. Of course, this will not happen all at once, but in a process that will unfold in stages.

What you must do, then, is to spend about ten minutes a day under the sun's rays, "breathing" them through the crown chakra and say these words:

"The sun is my home. The sun is my spirit. The sun is my creation. The electro-magnetic energy enters all strata of my body and soul and is well assimilated in all the cells and in all the foundations of my creation. Here I AM. I AM connecting to the information streaming and flowing to me."

Take a deep breath and begin to transfer your energy to your body. When the crown chakra begins to awaken, connect to the yellow flame, to Lord Lanto[8], and begin to assimilate the codes.

---

8 *Lord Lanto is the master of the second flame, the flame of divine wisdom.

The Third Code: The Third Eye Chakra

The chakra of the third eye is an energy center that was blocked during the falling of the souls. This energy center is a ball of energy punctured with tiny holes, each hole the size of a pinpoint. In entities who meditate, the third eye opens and they can see beyond time, space, and dimensions. They can see the infinite, and what exists in God's creation.

Today, the third eye is enormous, and from time to time it opens in some of you; but energetic blockages in your lives and in the lives of those around you prevent it from remaining open. In order for it to open, you must be in clean and pure surroundings. When you are in the fifth dimension, the third eye will open in order to reinforce your personal journey on the path of light and you will see through this chakra. That is how life will be conducted.

Dear ones, imagine a ray of light the color of indigo blue, flowing from the divine source into the third eye chakra. See the ray penetrating all the fine pinholes of the ball, and how every said point opens to the light of creation. Perform this activity for six days until you see that all the pinpoints are open, and say the following words:

"**The eye is the mirror of the soul. The eye is the door to divine light. The eye is the door to All That Is in the universes in which I exist. The eye will open in harmony to the masculine and feminine energies becoming One with the development and growth of my soul. Open. Open. Be Open and See.**"

The Fourth Code: the Throat Chakra

Dear ones, we are entering the sacred heart and providing details about the codes reaching us and undergoing preparation in the frequency so that we will be able to transmit them to you, sons of light, dear human beings.

The fourth code works on the throat chakra. Throughout the day, this energy center emits frequencies containing molecules of a positive or negative charge, passing among human beings and absorbing into your bodies. As of today, many human beings are not aware of the negative charge coming out of their mouths, and what an effect it has on those around them. Hence, there is great importance to this chakra and to the use of the frequencies emerging from it.

Look and notice how a ball built from a crystalline grid surrounds the energy center of the throat chakra. The crystalline ball absorbs all the negative frequencies emitted from their mouths, while the positive frequencies become more powerful as they pass through the crystal grid to the space of energy in which you exist. Thus, the positive connects to the light and can contain your being in the third dimension.

Repeat the following words, and see how fast and great the effect is:

"**My throat is an energetic refuge that influences the enlightenment of the environment in which I exist. My throat emits the positive words, and the crystalline grid absorbs the negative energy in negative words. Ah ooh ah, Ah ooh ah, Ah ooh ah.**"

The Fifth Code: the Heart Chakra

At this time, we are connecting to you, human beings on the surface, you who live and breathe life in a direct connection with Mother Earth.

Indeed, the connection will continue, but the way things happen will change. In this period, you are learning, remembering and arousing again the chakras that activate your physical body at any given moment. You must be aware that without this energetic center, both your etheric body and your physical body will lose their absolute balance.

I am focusing on the heart chakra. It is situated in the center of the body in a place that balances all its components. Understand that this energetic center is the activation center of your body in connection with the higher self, the Creator, the angels, the guides, and all existence above the third dimension. In most human beings, the center is still dormant, hence this chakra is being activated in stages. At this time, most human beings on the surface of the planet are awakening and each in his own way is finding the connection to the heart chakra.

The heart chakra is the chakra through which you are asked to think and feel. Thinking through the heart, then, is done by illuminating the area and by renewing and expanding the chakra. In some of you, there is a crystal within the chakra, constituting the energetic center. Accordingly, you must connect with the crystal found in your sacred heart and make sure it is charged with the energy of love for the sake of humanity and for the sake of nature—living and inanimate—on Planet Earth. You must think, understand, experience through the heart, and listen to one another.

The role of the energy passing through the present place is to awaken the dormant place from which sons of Lemuria operated on the mother continent. The heart is the central place. It leads in creation, in action, in intention and from it, the other parts of the body operate in synchronization. When the heart is blocked, there is no connection among the chakras, which causes the state of obtuseness and eye-closing familiar to you.

Therefore, dear ones, breathe into the heart the pink ray of Paul the Venetian. Enter your heart, and say:

"My heart is your heart. Your heart is my heart. We are All One."

Imagine your heart illuminating the planet and connecting to the tens of thousands of hearts already in the light. The connection gives you the feeling that everything is one and that you are one with all the open hearts on the planet. Sensitivity to those around you has increased ten-thousand-fold, and the giving, the support, and desire to help the nameless—are changing. There is an openness of hearts. This is the Messianic Age.

The Sixth Code: the Chakra of the Solar Plexus

The solar plexus chakra is the chakra of awakening. It is the place that is responsible for waking up to the choice of taking responsibility; a place from which you operate in agreement with divine will. The solar plexus illuminates the area between the navel and the heart. This is the area that supports the network/grid of chakras for balance, and in your body, it is like a sun sending its yellow-orange rays. When it is at its best, balanced, you feel vibrant, alert, and open to forming your creation.

In order to illuminate the center, say the following words:

"I AM That I AM—awakening to the enlightenment of divinity. I AM That I AM—choosing to take responsibility. I AM That I AM—full of creation and enlightenment. The center is BALANCED. BALANCED. BALANCED."

Indeed, it is important to keep this center balanced. Perform this illumination every morning.

The Seventh Code: the Sacral Chakra

Peace, dear ones. The time is the time of Nebuel, the god of prophecy, the time of fulfillments. At this time, sons of light have the ability to receive immense knowledge from the fifth dimension. The new knowledge will be assimilated into your physical body and you, dear ones, will be able to use it both in your light work and in the connection between the fifth and third dimension.

The sacral chakra is situated in a very sensitive part of your body, between the solar plexus and the root. This chakra helps you carry out processes and make correct choices in your life. The information that exists in the chakra is ancient information that is awakening, and the chakra is being charged anew every day.

In the center of the chakra, there exists a magnet that will help you magnetize what is familiar to you—like attracts like. With the help of this place, you can create for yourselves reality in the third dimension according to the energy you summon.

At this time, with the reinforcement of the magnetic grid that exists around the planet, the chakra is strengthened and you feel precisely which people you should meet and cooperate with in the third dimension, while the sacral chakra causes you to reject other people with whom the connection does not transform your energy. The chakra is charged and becomes fully balanced when your body illuminates the protons and the electrons by means of intensive sport, rapid breathing, and meditation in the fifth dimension.

When the chakra is open and the magnet is charged, your recognition ability is greatly enhanced and your choices are correct and not erroneous.

The sacral chakra is situated between the root place, Mother Earth, and the place of the spirit. Indeed, this chakra has guided you many times to balance between being grounded in the third dimension and ascended in the fifth dimension.

At this time, the chakra is reopening in order to continue supporting the balance that will bring the spirit from the fifth dimension to the third dimension. This chakra is yellow and shining, nourished by the energy of the central sun, growing more powerful and spreading its vibrations to the other chakras in your physical body.

Observe the energy that spreads from this chakra to the lower part of your body and then to the upper part. Breathe deeply and say the following words:

"I AM balanced between the spiritual and the material. I AM balanced between the earthly and the divine. I AM balanced between the old and the new. I

AM balanced between the two sides of the creation. This balance accompanies all the energy centers in my body."

Be open and attentive to the sacral chakra. Breathe it in, and with its help decide upon your path.

The Eighth Code: the Sex Chakra

The sex chakra, also called the root chakra, is the root energy of the human race. It is the link to the energetic base and constitutes the link with the material and density of the body, with Mother Earth, with the present energetic state from which human beings arise and develop spiritually.

This chakra provides many human beings with the ancient human balance in connection to the earth, which is the connection to the energy of life and the energy of creation. Through this center of energy, human beings undergo the only divine experience that has been preserved in their body with the decline in consciousness and in the divine connection—an experience in which the body receives life energy that is sometimes wasted.

Dear ones, when you join with bodies that you do not respect, purely for pleasure and not for a higher purpose— energy flows from the energy center that causes pleasure, but this is momentary and unbalances you for a long period of time. When human beings are constantly in an unbalanced state and their happiness is momentary, they are trapped in a circle of illusions. You must understand that only after a connection has been made at the level of the higher chakras, should you come into contact with the root or sex chakra, exchange energies between bodies and enrich one another. If you do this, at the end of the encounter there will be divine balance like nothing you have felt before. The purpose of the balance is to heal the body and to continue to act from the higher soul source of consciousness for the sake of enlightenment. Therefore, dear ones, in your next meeting with energy connected to the sex chakra, examine carefully whether or not the connection is vital and whether or not it arises from the essence of love and wholeness.

In order to connect to the next two chakras, the gold chakra and the silver chakra, and to receive the codes you must be fully conscious at the level of balance of the frequencies.

The next chakras, high chakras, are open and can be worked with at this time with the connection to divine will, with the lifting of the veil, with the preparation of the crystal bodies and with the joining of our bodies. After balancing and working with all the chakras, you must ask the "I AM" about readiness for work with the two high chakras in order to form a deep connection at the highest level of consciousness.

The Ninth Code: the Silver Chakra

The silver chakra is situated above the kingdom chakra, high above the planet, and is intended for those enlightened human beings who choose to ascend.

This chakra awakens after work has been done, after illumination of all the centers in the physical-etheric body and connection to the kingship chakra has been made. With enlightenment, it transmits energies from the source of the Creator to the son of light. Sons of light who channel are connected to this chakra that is open in them. The silver chakra must be absolutely balanced and its protection is energetic, in the shape of a diamond that surrounds and protects it from energies that are not beneficial to it. Many times, the chakra is guarded by angels, and is activated as long as the son of light continues the journey to enlightenment and has a consciousness of love and compassion.

Only in a state of activation of these frequencies will the chakra continue to be connected to the other chakras in the energetic center of the son of light.

The more connected the son of light is to the fifth dimension, the more harmoniously the information and the connection between the dimensions will run. The fifth dimension will gradually accelerate the son of light and the third dimension will be swallowed.

To activate the chakras, the son of light must be connected with his higher self, washing and purifying the bodies, and connecting with personal guidance. Only in a pure state can you declare:

"**I AM a son/daughter of the kingdom. I AM a son/daughter of the heavens. I AM the One who is joined to the essence of cosmic energy. I AM the One who is joined to the Whole. I AM open to the reunion of the Divine Self, ONE. ONE. ONE.**"

The Tenth Code: the Gold Chakra

The gold chakra is situated in that place where your entity is joined to the One and the union, the place where you are ascending masters, possessing the ability to connect with the Creator. For the most part, in this place you are in a state of out-of-body ascension and understand in an absolute way the choice of the soul. The connection with the gold chakra will exist after a process of full awareness, in the way of the masters. The connection to this energetic center raises you to an alchemical state so that you will completely disappear from the third dimension.

Peace

A gentle frequency of love, a gentle frequency of harmony and unity—this is what is needed in order for peace to exist in the Middle East. For thousands of years, this area has been given to disputes, blood, and tears. Many souls have come to the region in the knowledge that the time of their incarnation will be brief and that they will sacrifice themselves. But, dear ones, with the changes occurring at this time, the time of peace is closer than it has ever been. The planet, which has entered a process of awakening in the past thirty years, has led to a softening of the darkness and a softening of the control and aggression that have existed in the region. And so, dear ones, the time has come for a new Planet Earth.

The energetic washing for the opening of the channel through which the energy enters will be performed by a group of human beings who will gather for a unique purpose: to conduct the energy into Mother Earth causing a deep energetic cleansing from the energies that the planet Gaia has absorbed over the past five thousand years. The cleansing will be performed in a number of locations in the land of Israel, a region that constitutes an important point of light, and will be carried out in the juncture between the energy of creation and the crystal bodies of human beings.

Indeed, dear ones, the energy that will enter the planet through your bodies will penetrate the core of Planet Earth, moving into the crystal nucleus located at the center. Planet Earth will contain the energy that enters, and stream it from the nucleus back out, distributing it to all the crystal centers located within the planet, which will contain it. The new energy has high frequencies. Therefore, in this process, the change of frequency will take place. The joining of living particles of the creation with light cells will create pure protons and electrons, and it is they that will build the new construction of frequencies in the planet.

Today, the frequency is already different and the new children absorb, see, and experience the different tempo of the planet, which is so rapid that the adult population in your world sometimes has difficulty adapting to it. With these vibrations, the change is coming about. Hearts are opening and the soul connects with the creation. The veil is raised, awakening in you many questions, the answers to which take you back to the divine source and return you to your sacred heart and to the inner peace within you.

The new energy will vibrate with vibrations of the fifth dimension and will go out again to the entire planet; and so, dear ones, the Middle East region will receive the critical mass of energy and begin the purification.

The juncture of the three continents—Africa, Asia, and Europe—is an important tectonic point. The most significant point in the purification process is the Gulf of Suez. This region, continuing all along the coast of the Gulf of Suez, constitutes an immense energetic portal that is opening at this time, and human beings who raise the frequency to the fifth dimension will be able to pass through it and travel in the expanses of time and space. This is a portal and vortex to other dimensions.

Indeed, dear ones, with the energetic change and the transformation of frequencies, the central sun will continue to distribute the frequencies of the divine spirit, which will enter the planet and wash the dark places. Dormant areas will awaken, and only those who can contain the new frequencies will continue on to the next phase of ascension.

Peace in the Middle East is close, and will indeed arrive. All the people of the Middle East will live in harmony and unity. The lack of water in the area will make you realize that only through unification of all the people can you survive in this region. Unification in the Middle East will be accomplished by those people who send the frequencies of their heart to those people in distress. Peace is the essential change and human beings will experience it at the level of the frequency of the fifth dimension. The inner peace that will reside in your sacred heart will bring about an essential change in all areas of your lives, and will spur peace among human beings all over the planet. The conflicts among the different tribes and among the various states will be resolved; even disputes between spouses will be resolved.

Indeed, these are Messianic days, days of harmony, unification, and peace. I bless you, dear ones. I am with you throughout the wonderful journey, the journey of ascension.

Adama

The Turquoise Flame: the Peace Flame

Welcome. Here I am, Adama, High Priest of Telos. I welcome you today, the day on which the connection to the divine will is taking place in your celestial being, connecting your "I AM" presence with the spark of divinity. These are very exciting days, days in which we are one; the veil is lifting, and the light is visible in your eyes.

Indeed, my dear ones, the turquoise flame, the celestial color, opens hearts and enables human beings to merge with divinity and freedom to raise their vibration. It is indeed one of the cosmic flames that holds within it the frequency of freedom, joy and love, opening the soul to the realms of angels. The mere connection with it grants serenity and peace. In these days when humanity is awakening and healing is deepening in the emotional bodies, you can work with this flame, for it carries within it the frequency of love, of the inner peace you all wish to achieve, peace that is created in love.

It is an inner peace that grows within you, from the connection to your soul to the "I AM" presence, a brave and loving connection to the high regions from whence you came into this life in your body and in your role. This is the flame that was carried by Gandhi and Miriam-Mary Magdalene; it is the flame that emanates from the lyrics of the songs sung during the 1960s and 1970s that bore the powerful frequency so vital in those days in preventing the collapse of the planet. John Lennon, whose songs—expressing the frequency of love, peace, and freedom—most of you relate to, carried this flame in his being and in his physical body.

It is a frequency that we feel and witness during this Golden Age, a frequency necessary in order to create a new reality in your world, a reality manifested in the frequency of joy in your hearts. It is the end of an era in which humanity has experienced pain in physical life and imbalance in the emotional life; it is an era in which human beings still act out of belligerence and ego, and walk in judgment with a closed heart.

Where is Joy?

The joy in your hearts is a healing frequency for all pain. Look at your children laughing; see how they know how to heal the world of adults with smiles and laughter. Do you remember how to activate the muscle of your mouth and laugh? Did you know that with the frequency of laughter in the body is bathed in the turquoise flame, expanding and recharging it with the light of the creator? In this way, dear ones, you open your hearts and healing commences. Much research has been done on smiling and laughter, and their impact on human beings. At this time, we are revealing to you that the turquoise flame supports this process and grants you this vibration in your light bodies and your emotional and physical bodies.

With the connection to this flame, you feel the nerve centers in your light bodies breathing, expanding, and awakening. Feel the flow of energy tingling in all the light points that make up your crystal bodies. The currents are transmitted as gentle pulses that enlighten every dormant cell. See how your way of thinking changes with the awakening of the bodies to the frequencies of laughter, harmony, and love. Thinking that creates a positive reality is building. Observe yourselves as you receive this new frequency of the turquoise flame.

While using the turquoise flame and learning anew to activate laughter, we are immunizing our bodies from disease, and raising the acceleration of fractal light particles. The Merkavah of Light[9] around our body resonates and protects us from any lower frequency that is not right for us. The turquoise flame is a flame of peace; it prevails in a shining temple, a temple that illuminates the skies of the planet above the islands of Greece. This temple creates the entryway to the inner tranquility that exists in your heart and in your being. With the connection to sea water and the murmuring of the waves, your body opens and you become aware of the existence of the flame in yourself. You feel the secrets in its layers; you feel the inner peace that comes from serenity, love, acceptance, and inclusion. Feel the

---

9 The "Merkavah of Light' is a vehicle of Ascension. It was believed in ancient times, and even written about by the Hebrews, that the merkavah could be turned on by certain principles in meditation. This involves breathing changes, and mind, heart, and body changes that alter the way a person perceives the reality.

connection with these frequencies. Look at the turquoise flame, refining and bestowing divine serenity in all your bodies when you are connected with its frequency.

The seven sacred flames, which emanate from the source of all that is, bathe Planet Earth and the sons of light, and provide the foundation for learning and correct uses of the forces of creation. We recently revealed two more flames, secret up to now, but that are available and recommended for you to use—the accelerating golden flame and the harmony flame, which combines gold, silver, and the white ray of ascension.

Today, we reveal to you the turquoise flame, which is the flame of peace; slowly but surely it is penetrating human hearts on Planet Earth, thus accelerating its action upon you. The crystals that carry the frequency of the turquoise flame are aquamarine, aqua aura, and Eilat stone[10]. We invite you to visit the crystal city above Mount Shasta and the temple of the turquoise flame. Let's take a deep breath and fill our body with the white glittering beam of light descending from the center of the universe. With it, our thoughts are cleared out of our physical, etheric, emotional, and mental bodies.

A multidimensional gateway is before us, and as we pass through it, we see a vast, beautiful field of flowers and trees; the animals welcome us. We walk in that field and hear a waterfall; the waterfall spills into to a big, beautiful pool surrounded by many plants and flowers. A huge rainbow

---

10 Eilat stone – it is a green-blue inhomogeneous mixture of several secondary copper minerals including malachite, azurite, turquoise, pseudomalachite, chrysocolla. The Eilat stone is the National stone of Israel, and is also known as the King Solomon Stone

with the colors of the flames crosses over the pool. We approach, dip our feet into it, and seeing that the water is warm and pleasant, we dive deep into the depths reaching its bottom. As we touch it, we see crystal colors glittering, the delicate turquoise color subtly illuminating our eyes. Now we are swimming, the oxygen continually cleansing our body, and we see a kind of shaft of light coming from the bottom of the pool. We swim into it and reach a beautiful cave built entirely of turquoise crystal. We get out of the water and go deep into the cave.

We discover different kinds of turquoise stone, and we feel the frequency of serenity entering our sacred heart. We walk, as if hovering, until we reach a huge dome built of clear quartz; at its center is an immense flame, the turquoise flame. The guardian of the flame arrives and welcomes us to the temple; he invites us to approach the flame; we do so, standing in front of it, reaching out our hands, breathing deeply, one... two... three... We feel the flame penetrating throughout our body. We feel serenity, love, and a sort of tickling that travels up our centers of energy bringing a smile to our lips and opening our hearts. We feel light, whole.

We see balloons of light floating toward us; with each balloon that approaches us, we send the frequencies of serenity, love, joy, and peace from our heart. The balloons float higher and higher until they leave through an opening at the top of the dome. The guardian of the flame invites the children of Telos, who have come today to be recharged with the frequency of the flame, to join our circle. The children are laughing. Listen to their rolling voices; listen to their laughter emerging from their loving hearts. The laughter is contagious and we too are laughing, laughing, laughing. Every laugh makes us feel that our body is picking itself up, rising up, and losing its weight. We are floating and laughing, immersed in the light.

After a few moments, we are relaxed; we thank the children of Telos. We are called back to the entrance of the cave. Once again, we enter the water, dive deep into the pool leaving through the beam of light. We see the beautiful vast field before us, leave the pool, and wrap ourselves in white robes.

We leave Telos, pass again through the inter-dimensional portal, and rejoin our physical body. We feel lightness, serenity, love, inner peace within our sacred heart.

(March 19th, 2013)

Inner Peace: A Message from Aurelia Louise Jones

Inner peace is a wonderful subject to work on at this time in our aspiration to achieve inner tranquility, tranquility that will lead us to a life of harmony and the natural flowing of our "I AM".

Indeed, dear ones, human beings awakening to the spiritual journey are aware of the lessons on which they need to work. These lessons raise ancient memories from within our being; hence fears also often arise concerning things we experienced as human beings in ancient times. The personality of human beings is influenced by the complexity of the soul and its incarnations on the planet. When you, human beings, deal with situations that push your personality into unpleasant places, feelings like pressure, tension, fear, and paralyzing anxiety arise from the subconscious—feelings stemming from imbalance of the soul. Treatment of these feelings through conscious work and departure from old habits can bring about softening and balance.

How do I know? How can I neutralize the fears that arise? Fear is not reality, it is an illusion. When you are in a state of great fear or loss of control, connect to the frequency of love and creation, to prayer, to music and to meditation. These will neutralize the fear. Consciously make friends with your fears, pave yourself a new road, pleasant and harmonious, free of fear.

Practicing a new reality is the way, practicing positive thinking, practicing considered action, practicing enlightenment of the bodies, practicing conscious living. In these times, there are many opportunities to learn, to acquire means to cope. This is a Messianic Age and these are the times to create inner peace within yourselves, peace that leads you deep into your personal journey and summons the light to your lives, peace that creates balance among mankind. From this inner peace will come outward peace.

When I wrote my last book, I realized that I must let go of many blockages, and that only when I succeeded in letting them go would I reach harmonious balance. Sadly, before I was able to do that, I became ill and the many karmas that were condensed into my being were liberated through the illness. The rapid liberation caused my body a great deal of suffering. Yes, dear ones, releasing anger and trauma is very important and we must learn to release them in order to prevent illness in our physical body.

With the frequency of love, it is possible to dissolve these dark places. The frequency of love is the frequency of life in Telos, and in the temples of healing in Telos it is possible to illumine the parts that still need healing. Now is the right time for work of this kind and you are invited to do it.

When I reached the other side of the veil and connected with my light body in the fifth dimension, I needed treatment to balance the frequencies and to heal my being from the hardship and suffering my physical body had undergone. Indeed, after awhile, I reconnected to my being from the fifth dimension with a happy memory of my soul sequence from the day I was created.

The energy in your dense body needs a great deal of light, hence there is great importance in daily meditations, working with wonderful consciousness and connecting with the light. These days, time is accelerating so greatly that you can feel it. This reality is meant to arouse you to life here and now without needless preoccupation with future or past. When you are connected to the present reality, your being is focused on the changes it must undergo. Therefore, dear ones, at every point in time where your being is, with all your bodies joined together as one, look inward, balancing your sacred heart and your energy centers, and you will achieve emotional balance. Be in consciousness, for from within consciousness will come ascension.

Yes, dear ones, the desire for ascension exists in all the strata of your soul. Your high choice, which arose from strong desire, was to grasp these days, at this point in time of humanity, a point in time that indicates a change of frequencies across the planet.

For your wonderful path, I, the beloved masters, the High Priest Adama, and all the Council of Light thank you. We support you and extend a hand to help with the deep healing you are undergoing and experiencing. Out of this healing and this inner peace, humanity will ascend to a new planet.

Yours, Aurelia

Glossary

Etheric body–The etheric body is like an invisible copy of the physical body. It is sensitive, vulnerable, and influenced by our thoughts and emotions, both positive and negative. Illnesses and disabilities are first manifested in the etheric body, and eventually permeate the physical body. The etheric body supports and provides energy to the different divisions of the physical body, and controls the assimilation processes. It repairs damage to the physical body caused by the tension in which we live in the density of the third and fourth dimensions. With the etheric body, we can fly and cross the borders of time and space in astral journeys.

Hierarchy–The hierarchy of the governing system of the stars and galaxies, from the council to the individual sections on the planets. The government hierarchy is constructed in depth, not in the familiar pyramid form. In the government hierarchy, there are many masters, archangels, and light beings, each of whom fills an important function in the creation.

Flames—The cosmic flames are the flames of the creation, which emerge from the center of the universe, from the source of all that is. They have unique and multicolored characteristics containing frequency, and some of the characteristics act on the human body, and in this way help balance the energy centers. The flames work with all the bodies—the etheric, the physical, the emotional, the mental, and the spiritual; they balance the energy centers in a state of imbalance, penetrate all the components of the bodies, and reinforce the frequencies in need of it. An ascended master oversees each flame and the role it performs on the planet. There is also a temple that represents each flame on the planet.

When one works daily with the flames, they assist in balancing the bodies, allowing for inner purification and pure thinking from your sacred heart. On the path to ascension, the flames support and enrich, and in continuous work with them, we purify our body on the way to ascension to the frequency of the fifth dimension.

The flame of wisdom and enlightenment—resonates in shades of yellow.
The flame of divine will—resonates in shades of blue.
The flame of love—resonates in shades of pink.
The flame of healing—resonates in shades of emerald green.
The flame of ascension—resonates in pure white, and contains the vibration of all the other flames.
The flame of rebirth—resonates gold, like the colors of sunset.

The fame of transformation—resonates in shades of violet.

Master—a person familiar with the truth and grace present around him in the physical world and in the spiritual world; a person who understands in his heart, in thankfulness, that the only duality that exists is that between being awake and being in a state of delusion.

The fifth dimension—this is the dimension with the high, ethereal frequency, containing the energy of love, compassion, harmony, and giving; the energy of the Creator. The connection with the Creator in this dimension is constant, and the balance is absolute.

At this time, when there exists the possibility of passing among the dimensions, many sons of light are coming to visit in the fifth dimension. With the ascension to the fifth dimension, our body changes; the bodies are refined into crystal bodies, and the DNA expands to thirty-six helices, as it was at the beginning of our path as humans.

Capabilities in the fifth dimension are tremendous; the essence of creation and experience exist in the frequency of love.

Carriage—also called "body light"; it is a structure made of two triangles placed opposite one another to create a three-dimensional Star of David. Operating the carriage makes it possible to transfer the consciousness to higher dimensions in astral travel, while the body remains in the third dimension and safeguards our etheric bodies.

The Akashic Library—an etheric library that contains the Akashic records; a universal system of recording in which there is infinite information connected with all the creation in the universe. All thoughts are recorded in it, all words and actions, all talents and all knowledge. Although many see the Akashic records as books and scrolls, they are not; in fact, they are made of energetic oscillations translated into pictures, shapes, symbols, images, and languages that the intelligence can understand. The records are accessible to anyone with regard to information related to themselves.

The Lemurian Age—from 4,500,000 to 12,000 years ago, there existed a very large continent called Lemuria. On this continent, the beings lived in absolute balance with nature, formed and created, lived in harmony, and filled their lives with a frequency of love, the frequency of the fifth dimension; in the Lemurian Age there existed a harmonious passage between the dimensions.

Some 26,000 years ago, a struggle developed between the civilization of Atlantis and Lemuria, regarding the right to enslave undeveloped cultures that existed in the third dimension. The Lemurians believed in the right of these cultures to freedom, while the Atlanteans thought otherwise. Thus, after a period of war, the darkness spread and the continent of Lemuria sank overnight, without the knowledge of the members of the civilization that inhabited it. Several priests and masters knew what was about to happen and created the light city Telos in the fifth dimension, in order to preserve the Lemurian tradition.

The Light City Telos—with the sinking of the continent, the survivors reached Telos. The city was built in the frequency of the fifth dimension, and began to create itself. Gradually temples and residences were built in it, the economy developed, and life was formed in the frequency of the fifth dimension. Today, the city is full of life; sons of light from the entire planet come to us for treatment, learning, initiation, and consecration. We have opened the heart of our portal to human beings, and today many receive the call to come visit the light city Telos and to create in the frequency of the fifth dimension—creation from the heart, from the heart of Telos.

The Pleiades—a cluster of several hundred stars located light years away from Planet Earth, which can be seen with a telescope. The Pleiadians are our ancient forbears; they resemble us and saw themselves as empowering Planet Earth and preparing it for life in the fifth dimension, the frequency of love, the frequency of creation. At this time, the Pleiadians are returning to the planet in order to gather information and extend to human beings their caressing hand that supports the process of awakening. "We are one in our image, we are one in our heart, we are one in our love."

Chakra—Chakra is the Sanskrit word for wheel. The chakras are rotating vortices of energy, centers that radiate the energy of the life force. There are seven main chakras in the physical body, located along the spine. There are also secondary chakras distributed on the surface of the body.

Each of the main chakras relates to a gland in the body and contains the quality of divine consciousness, through one of the seven rays, and controls a specific area of earthly experience.

The central sun—The central sun is the source of the creation, the source of life. It is situated at the center of the universe and transmits energetic frequencies to the universe and to parallel universes; it sends the frequency to Planet Earth and thus greatly influences human beings as well. The central sun vibrates with the frequency of the twelfth dimension and illuminates the planets that exist in many universes; it is the source of creation and the source of life.

Vortex portal—in the universe in which the solar system of Planet Earth exists, which is one of many, there exist energetic portals, vortex portals. The vortices create possibilities of entering and exiting between dimensions and between universes; the vortex portal is entered through a sleeve that takes the traveler a distance of hundreds of light years from place to place. Travel in time and space has no connection with time and space as human beings define them. In fact, there is no time, and there is no space. Travel in the vortex makes possible those free beings unlimited in time and space.

Aurelia Louise Jones—received the keys to the city of Telos, and wrote three books about the light city Telos, as well as a book about the sacred flames. Her book about the knowledge was channeled to her by the High Priest Adama. She even conducted journeys of ascension in the mountain, guided by Adama—these journeys continue to take place within the framework of world Telos organizations. Following the information imparted in her enchanting books, world Telos organizations have been established, whose goal it is to arouse humanity spiritually, to reach the world of unity in which peace, tranquility, harmony, unconditional love, and beauty prevail; a world in which there is unity among all races, nations, and religions; a world in which all make up one big family. Today Telos organizations are active in Japan, Australia, England, the United States, Canada, France, Finland, Denmark, and Israel.

The Telos Organizations around the world were inspired by the late Aurelia Louise Jones, author of The Telos Book Series and The Seven Sacred Flames. These organizations derive their name from the City of Telos, a Lemurian City of Light in the fifth dimension, part of the Cities of Light network within the earth which lies beneath Mount Shasta, CA in the USA. The city was created by Lemurian survivors after the continent sank over 12,000 years ago. The Telos organizations around the world continue to support Aurelia's work and spread the messages of the Lemurian light, passing on messages from the Masters, led by Adama, the high priest of Telos. The organization's goal is to inspire humanity spiritually. We want to reach a world that exists in peace, tranquility, harmony, unconditional love, and beauty; a world in which there is unity among all races, nations and religions, a world where we are all one big family.

The late Aurelia Louise Jones wrote and self-published books filled with her knowledge and wisdom, with messages from Adama and the masters of Telos, providing us with many tools that we can utilize in all areas of our lives, both physically and spiritually.

Books published to date are:
- *Telos, Volume 1 Revelations of the New Lemuria*
- *Telos, Volume 2, Messages for the Enlightenment of Humanity in Transformation*
- *Telos, Volume 3 Protocols of the Fifth Dimension*
- *The Seven Sacred Flames*
- *The Ascension Flame of Purification and Immortality*
- *Prayers to the Seven Sacred Flames*
- *Angelo's Message: Angelo the Angel Cat Speaks to All People on This Planet*

The Effects of Recreational Drugs on Spiritual *Development*

Publisher: Mount Shasta Light Publishing

The Telos Israel Organization is a branch of the Telos World Organization founded by the late Aurelia Louise Jones.

The world organization follows the path of Aurelia in spreading the Lemurian light, through messages from the masters, headed by Adama, the High Priest. The purpose of the organization is to awaken humanity spiritually. We aspire to a world of unity in which peace, tranquility, harmony, unconditional love, and beauty prevail. A world in which there exists unity among all races, nations, and religions, a world in which we all constitute one big family. It is our aspiration to expand the Lemurian family circle in Israel, and to expose as many as possible to the tradition, the teachings, and the pearls of Lemurian wisdom. With their help, applying the tools we have been provided, we will live in a better world, we will learn to respect, to love unconditionally, to give, to devote ourselves, to share, and to contribute to the community. We send you blessings of light and love, Telos Israel

Books published by Ayelet Segal

- *Telos, From Theory to Practice, A Voyage On The Way To Ascension.*
- *Back to Telos, The Adventures of Oraion, In Telos, The Lemurian City of Light"*

These books are based on information and messages received from the high priest of Telos, Adama, and other masters and spiritual teachers in Telos, the City of Light. They are full of pure love for mankind, and exude a strong desire to share the divine wisdom, which is a way of life for the Lemurian people in Telos. This book, *The Adventures of Oraion, In Telos, The Lemurian City of Light*, was written to help those children who are in the process of ascension and spiritual growth. We strive to expand the Lemurian family circle across the world, to reveal the Lemurian heritage, knowledge, and wisdom to as many people as we can. With their help and while using the tools provided to us, we will live in a better world. We are learning to respect, love unconditionally, share, and contribute to the community.

Heart-to-heart, the worldwide Telos family.

For more information,

Look for the Telos organization in your country.

About Ayelet Segal

Mother of Ori, Ziv, Tamar and Ohad, Indigo, Crystal and Rainbow beloved children. MA in education, a teacher, a holistic psychotherapist, group facilitator, Telos organization representative in Israel. Human being walking on an awakening journey.

"The journey to Telos takes place on a path of absolute faith, a path on which the connection to the sacred heart is essential, a path on which one deals with challenging lessons. Today I am aware how far those lessons have taken me on my personal spiritual journey, as well as on my journey as part of Telos-Israel."

I see myself on a mission to spread the vibration of Lemuria, the vibration of the heart, and out of personal connection and work with Indigo, Crystal and Rainbow children, I felt the call from the city of light Telos to the children of the world. This is how I started the journey of Oraion, The Crystal Child, through which we learn the laws of the fifth dimension, the way of love and light, and get tools with which we can deal with the world of the third dimension. Dispel density and dramas, love from the head, and think from the heart...

Made in the USA
Middletown, DE
11 August 2019